Journey To Your Soul
The Angels' Guide to Love and Wholeness

$$\varphi$$

CAROLE MARLENE SLETTA

NANCY AMBROSE SNODGRASS

And Their
Angels

CAMERON and TOM

The Angels' Handbook for Humans - Book 1

White Phoenix Publishing
Lake Oswego, Oregon

Printed in the United States of America

Graphic design by Design Studio Selby

Editor, Cheryl Long Riffle

Library of Congress Cataloging-in-Publication Data

Sletta, Carole Marlene, 1942-
    Journey to your soul: the angels guide to love and
wholeness/Carole Marlene Sletta, Nancy Ambrose Snodgrass;
and their angels Cameron and Tom.
        p. cm. -- (The angels handbook for humans; bk. 1)
    ISBN 1-889190-00-4 (pbk.)
    1. Angels. 2. Spiritual life. 3. Church renewal--Catholic
Church--Miscellanea. 4. Sletta, Carole Marlene, 1942-
5. Snodgrass, Nancy Ambrose, 1949- 6. Cameron (Spirit)
7. Oddo, Thomas (Spirit) 8. Catholic Church--History--
1965--Miscellanea. I. Snodgrass, Nancy Ambrose, 1949-.
II. Cameron (Spirit) III. Oddo, Thomas (Spirit) IV. Title.
V. Series.
BL477.S57 1997   97-13366
242.4'82--dc21   CIP

White Phoenix Publishing
P.O . Box 2157, Lake Oswego, Oregon 97035
503-639-4549

FIRST EDITION
97 98 99 2000 01 /10 9 8 7 6 5 4 3 2 1

Contents

Prologue *7*

Preface *9*

Introduction *11*

1   The Beginning *17*

2   Embracing Oneself *23*

3   Allowing the Truth to Be Spoken *29*

4   Truth Wears Many Masks *37*

5   Pedestal Not Sacred *47*

6   Soul Bonding Is Possible *57*

7   Bonding in the Eyes Comes With Caution . . *67*

8   Arming Oneself With Light *75*

9   Peace Within You Becomes Apparent *81*

10 Miracles Become Your Companion *95*

11 Circle With Two Sides Becomes Proper . . . *107*

12 Opposites Can Only Be the Same *123*

13 Do We Die to Come Back? *137*

14 Do We Choose Our Own Path? *151*

15 For Now We Say Goodbye *163*

Acknowledgments

Love to my wonderful husband, Ron, children, Kimberely, Teresa, Stephen, Heather, and Michael., grandchildren ,Christopher, Ashley, Jacob, Joshua, and baby Madeline. They have always been a pillar of strength for me, especially when I needed them the most.

To my incredible friends who inspired me to continue on with this book when I became fearful. And to my therapists who encouraged me with such love and caring compassion. They were able to pull me out of my deepest despair and show me I was precious when I felt so worthless. Bless them for their superior guidance.

Carole

To my many angels on earth, who appear as my sons Nate and Matt, relatives, friends, therapists, spiritual teachers and neighbors for their support, love, and belief in me. Without you the words would not have become a book, and the love within me would not be as deep. My gratitude is immeasureable.

Nancy

We would both like to thank Tani Douglass for typing our manuscript, Robert Selby, Miriam Selby, and B.J. Schmeltzer for their technical help and Cheryl Long Riffle for believing in us and for editing and publishing our book.

This book is dedicated to

our divine Angels

Cameron and Tom

Prologue

This book is about two women who, together with their angels, went on a spiritual journey to find their souls. They had only a glimpse of what was about to unfold as this path opened up to them.

Their paths became adventures with surprising twists and turns. And while the lessons they experienced were different for each of them, parallel's always existed. Their adventures led them both to the deeply hidden parts of their spiritual side and for one of them the revelation of a stunning and captivating love.

Carole's angel, Cameron, channeled his unconditional love and wisdom using her voice. These messages were tape-recorded and carefully transcribed.

Nancy's angel, Tom, came through her hand and brought his insightful hope for change in his beloved church and his desire for everyone to achieve a deeper level of loving.

It became profoundly apparent to the authors that the lessons they learned about unconditional love, as recorded in this book, were their most treasured gifts. This book is shared by the authors and intended by the angels for all who want to find their own soul's beauty and a pathway to wholeness and deeper loving.

Preface

Cameron

Cameron says he lived on earth over 200 years ago. He lived in India. His accent is heavy with broken English, and because of this, his words may need to be read with thought and deliberation for clarity. We also found that all the chapters build upon one another, therefore, the value of this book is enhanced when read from beginning to end.

He says he is coming to us as a male-female entity, with knowledge of his other lives. Cameron says the wisdom he speaks is a collection of many angels conferring. Often he states "we" in this book, thus giving credit to his guides. He is a most loving, gentle, and kind angel who proclaims not to have all the answers. Cameron says our answers are within each of us.

Acting upon Cameron's loving suggestion, Carole and Nancy have added their thoughts after each chapter and show how the lessons on love have helped them pave their paths of light.

Tom Oddo

*T*om Oddo led by walking beside people. He believed in allowing others to be the best they could be. Tom spent his entire life loving and giving to the people he touched.

His early years in Bayside, Long Island, were filled with organizing a boys swim club, serving as an alter boy, and helping around the rectory at his family's Catholic parish. By the time he graduated from Holy Cross High School, he knew he wanted to be a Holy Cross priest.

Undergradute years were spent at Norte Dame where he was awarded the Presidential Medal as one of sixteen students to have an impact on the university. He completed his masters degree in professional theology at Holy Cross College and at Catholic University of America in Washington, D.C. in 1969. One year later he was ordained a priest in the Congregation of Holy Cross.

For the next nine years he involved himself in his doctoral work at the Graduate School of Arts and Sciences at Harvard in religious studies. At the same time, he immersed himself in pastoral work among gay Catholics, peace workers, and the poor in Boston. Harvard awarded him a Ph.D. in Christian Philosophy in 1979.

Oddo received a full, tenured appointment as assistant professor in Religious Studies at Stone-hill College, Massachusetts. In 1982 he was chosen to be the seventeenth president of the University of Portland in Oregon. "He had something special that we all sensed, an agape love that one associates with people like Mother Teresa," stated a selection committee member. Tom was just thirty-eight years old when he became president. For seven years he led with optimism, sensitivity, charisma, and love. He believed in consensus building and sharing leadership with those around him. The university flourished. Then on October 26, 1989 Tom Oddo was killed at the age of forty-five when his car was hit by a runaway trailer.

Introduction

Carole

*M*y search for the light began with much darkness. I believe I asked for parents to teach me many hard lessons. The main one being self-love. They did this in such a way that from infancy on I was searching for approval.

Because I was not nurtured at home and some of my needs were not met, I relied on myself. I grew up in nice homes, in desirable neighborhoods with an abundance of material possessions. Everything appeared perfect to an onlooker. However, the most important needs that I sought, to feel loved and special, were lacking. Later I understood that my parents could not teach confidence and self-love to a child when they had none themselves.

The Catholic church was very important to our family so, of course, I was reared accordingly. I sometimes felt comfort in being able to confide to a special nun about home secrets, but by the look on her face I discovered these were things that should stay that way—secret! After telling, it was not long before I was switched to another school. I recall that this situation was repeated. When I was about eight years old, the effect of my telling family secrets brought such harsh consequences that I decided it best to remain silent. Anyway, my father said I was stupid and that people would not, and did not, believe me. I kept asking myself, "Will I ever get out of this? Why am I here? What is this all about? Who am I? What is my purpose?"

In spite of everything, my childhood seemed pretty normal to me at the time. I had learned to keep my thoughts and ideas to myself. But I wondered what it would be like to live where there was laughter, talking and sharing. Even though silence was drilled into me by my family, sharing with others was what my heart longed for.

My search for self has spanned over half a century. At

one point I concluded that everything that was wrong in my life could be cured if I JUST lost that extra twenty pounds. With that thought as my catalyst, I started on a relentless search for a miracle cure through the latest diet, new weight-loss gimmick, or "magic pill." This consumed much of my time. It worked for awhile but somehow the weight always became a part of me again.

One day a woman I knew handed me a business card with a therapist's name on it. I believe she was an angel of sorts. I had no idea why I would want to go to a therapist. But an inner push led me to make an appointment. Arriving at the therapist's office, I was greeted by a most loving woman. I immediately felt safe with her. She became my primary therapist.

I felt normal as I sat down in her office. When she asked about my life, I found that I had no deep feelings about it, in fact I felt rather numb. My life was okay. It seemed kind of dull, with little purpose. I guess in my mind, I had achieved a satisfactory level. I felt I was a good wife and had loved, cared, and protected my five children to the best of my ability. My grandchildren added so much love to our family that everything seemed complete. So why WAS I here? Ah, my weight issue. I soon learned, however, that the weight was my coverup for other unresolved issues. I put it on the back burner to be dealt with later.

The safety I felt with my primary therapist allowed me to continue without fear. Therapy lasted almost two years. Far into my healing two more gifted people helped me. Their approach to healing was different, yet complimentary. The therapists let me find my own truth. They gave me love and strength as I discovered all the hidden parts of myself. Without a doubt it was the hardest thing I have ever done! It was also the best gift I could ever have given myself!

Self discovery was amazing. Now I can have feelings, thoughts, and opinions. I can laugh, cry, be happy, sad, or even mad—a big one to give myself permission to do— and it's okay. I learned forgiveness. I like myself. I'm not stupid. What a revelation! I can do anything I choose. So many choices! The sky's the limit.

Finally my life seemed rich and full. Could it possibly get any better? Is there more to this mystery called life? Something was about to unfold . . . and then I met Nancy.

Nancy

I 'm very grateful for everything I have experienced in my life. Now every day love pours into me as my angels guide me. My life is exciting, full of love, and adventure. This book tells how I got here and how it happened.

On the outside, my childhood was envied by my friends. With a big house in the country, expansive lawns, a tennis court, and summers at our cabin by the lake, my four sisters and I appeared to have the perfect life.

Each summer I was at Girl Scout camp where singing was an important part of the experience. The music entered my soul and is still there today. In some respects music was an escape. Today when my sisters and I harmonize and remember the camp songs, the beautiful melodies embrace my being and take me back to those backpack and canoe trips. Nature became a haven where I felt safe. The beauty that existed all around me fed my soul and created a deep love and connection to the outdoors.

Back home I felt disharmony and sadness for my mother and father. It was in harsh contrast to the peaceful harmony of summer. My parents were two individuals whose destiny it was to be together and teach their five daughters many lessons. Now, as I look back, with fresh insight and wisdom, I can understand how this all worked. It was my choice to be with these parents who were unhappy. They presented me with the opportunity to learn how to be happy in an unhappy environment.

What was a child to do? Keep the secret and certainly do not admit to anyone how miserable life is at home. Worse yet, make sure everyone pretends that everything is fine. That was the beginning of my search for truth. Living in complete untruth turned out to be an enormous gift for me and for that I am grateful. What I developed through that experience was a desire to live in truth.

Graduation from a college was expected of me, so I dutifully obliged. Then I married a man I grew up with and we had two beautiful sons. Sensing an unsettled feeling inside of me, I eventually realized that I needed therapy. During those sessions memories surfaced about painful incidents in my childhood. Something led me through therapy and now I know that I was being guided by my inner soul and my angel. I began to open up and to trust more each day.

A gradual change seemed to empower me. As I learned how to express my feelings, I soon realized that my marriage was empty of intimacy and a deep exchange of feelings. When I approached my husband with my desire to have more intimacy and depth, I found he wanted something else. We went our separate ways. For many months afterward, my soul screamed in pain from the loss of the family. I then had to face the truth about my childhood and marriage. I vaguely remember asking God to help me. This is when my life really began.

My sister suggested that I see a counselor friend of hers, "Someone gifted," she said. I did. This was the beginning of my journey into another dimension. During one session the counselor suggested that I close my eyes and imagine being in a safe place. A vision of a meadow and brook with two angelic beings appeared. I walked up and hugged them. The love I felt with them was beyond anything I'd ever experienced. They spoke to me telepathically saying, "Nancy, you are a most beloved angel spirit. You are finally connecting with your highest knowing and purpose."

During the next four months I was continually "zapped" by an incredible force of light and love. This energy permeated my entire body. It actually pulsated through me. My draw was mostly to the male angel who became my close companion and friend. I believe God sent him to me for my healing. He taught me to trust and not be afraid. In addition, he was my catalyst to a profound spiritual awakening.

Life moved on quickly and more angels came to guide and love me. My growth came at lightening speed. The experiences were profound, exciting, and astonishing. I evolved from a person who just two years ago never really believed in God, to one who knows beyond a doubt that there is an enormous force of love and light guiding us. My belief is that it is God, our Creator.

My soul hungered to learn more as I sensed this was just the beginning. Somewhere deep within me was the belief that I was about to take another huge leap . . . and then I met Carole.

ONE

The

Beginning

Nancy

*W*ho could have guessed the impact a simple experience in eavesdropping would have on my life. On a beautiful, warm October day in 1993 while watching my son's soccer game, I became aware of a conversation going on behind me. Two women were talking about the great Sunday service at my church. I leaned back to say I had been there too and agreed. Carole was one of the women, and her son was on the same newly-formed soccer team as my son. Carole and I soon became lost in deep conversation, stopping only long enough to watch our sons make their plays on the field. Carole shared that she felt safe with me and was now in therapy over some difficult childhood issues. She had told very few people and was really feeling isolated and alone. Carole said she felt comfortable with me. I told her that I had completed my own therapy not too long ago for similar issues. She said it was good to meet someone who understood and spoke the same language.

My sense was that I could help Carole get in touch with her angels and I was being guided to assist her. I offered to help her meet her angels. As my awareness has grown, I realize nothing is by chance. The experience was to become a lesson in feeling the truth. How valuable for us on our journey into other dimensions.

That first experience began as I took Carole through a visualization exercise, the same one I had experienced when I connected with my angels. She said that she felt completely safe. Closing her eyes, she settled into the beautiful visions and began to feel a presence. She saw a figure standing by a brook; he said his name was Dean. Soon I could hear halting words come out of Carole. Then the words became sentences. I knew Carole was channeling Dean's voice. This very masculine voice had many loving messages for us. He was mainly here to help Carole with her self-love and belief in herself. We met several times to help her get in touch with Dean and receive his messages.

This was the opening for Carole's awareness to her guides. After awhile she began to sense that another angel wanted to speak through her. One day, while she was channeling, an angel named Lilly began to speak. Her voice and personality were totally different from Dean's. Lilly became our weekly, sometimes daily, companion for two months. She made predictions about the future and told us exactly what our lives would be like, which sounded exciting and fun. For two months we followed along before becoming suspicious that this was not a totally enlightened presence. We began to feel that Lilly was not promoting our highest growth. We both felt strong enough to decide that we would have nothing to do with Lilly anymore.

Looking back, we see what a great learning experience that was. It developed "street smarts" for us as well as caution and discretion. We realized that we had been allowing someone else to run our lives. Neither people nor angels should be allowed to do this. Strong and empowered, we resolved never to let this happen again. I thought it was interesting that I learned this valuable lesson from an angel rather than a person.

We decided to stay away from this "angel stuff " for awhile. It was like being burned in a relationship and retreating into a cave to heal your wounds. That's exactly what we did. It took a long time to finally realize how valuable this experience was and how much it taught and strengthened us. It taught us to feel truth.

Approximately five months later, I told Carole that I would like to try again. She agreed. We were drawn to the love and lessons that can come from angels. Somehow we knew that we needed help to protect ourselves. In researching, I learned that there are earthbound angels who are not for our highest soul advancement. They have their own growth and healing to do, and they will use us if we allow it. Since then, I've heard numerous stories of humans who have allowed earthbound angels to take over their lives. We have free will; we should never allow anyone to do this to us. We are in control of our lives, no one else. It has been my observation that people who don't have much self-love are more easily influenced. This had been true for us. Lilly had come to us during a vulnerable time. I was recently divorced and questioned every aspect of my self-worth. Carole was also in a space needing self-love.

We learned to say a prayer of protection every time we channeled, and bless the angels who help us. It is necessary to be extremely cautious. However, once the precautions are taken care of, the rewards are unbelievable.

Feeling strong, we were ready to try again. An entirely new and loving entity came through Carole. He introduced himself as Cameron. She had been hearing his name for sometime.

Cameron was completely different from Lilly and spoke in a somewhat broken English accent. He explained that he was called in to protect us, and if we chose, to guide us. Therein lies the difference between earthbound and more highly evolved angels. Cameron always states, "If you choose." He refuses to tell us the outcome of any situation or predict the future. Many times I've tried to get it out of him. Cameron says we have total control and choice in our lives, and he explained that he was here to help us find our own inner guidance and learn to find the answers by listening to our own souls. The wisdom and love he expressed was beautiful. He explained that all the answers to all our questions are within us. We were soon to learn how to find these answers. What a glorious adventure!

Carole channeled Cameron for over a year. During that year we learned incredible lessons and began to trust ourselves and our intuition. We began to believe that the wonderful messages we were receiving could be shared with others. We asked Cameron about this and he confirmed that information was available for a book if we chose and that he would assist us.

Our belief was that when we had evolved to a certain point, we would be ready to write a book. Our understanding of our evolution was in the areas of self-love, belief in ourselves, and trusting the guidance given. Cameron said he was called in for Carole's protection, healing, and for the healing of others. That year provided amazing lessons, guidance, and counseling as I encountered life's challenges.

Finally we knew we were ready for this book. Cameron explained that if we chose, we could tape his messages-lessons and then relate how we had applied that lesson to our lives. Carole and I soon observed that whatever the lesson, we had parallel circumstances happening in our lives to teach us. Whatever one of us was learning, very soon something would happen to the other in a different   form, but nevertheless, to teach the same lesson. This was fascinating as we compared incidents in our lives.

  We began to be observers as well as participants in our lives. Soon we were able to step out of ourselves, see the lessons, and then learn rather than being caught and stuck in it all. It was exciting and fun. Everyday brought something new. Even the lessons that were taught in pain were rewarding. Together we learned to trust that there is a grand design for our lives. We started letting go of our worries and knew that there was always a perfect reason for every occurance. Our love and immense gratitude grew for Cameron, our teacher and guide.

TWO

Embracing Self

Cameron

*W*e wish to begin by saying that we all start out as a wonderful beautiful seed of light that we must nurture and grow. Our purpose in this book is to help others find their beauty and divineness. There are many ways to do this. Everyone is conceived in love and conceived in beauty. But often what happens in a world with so many displeasures are that layers upon layers are wrapped around this beautiful seed of light. It is our wish for this book to assist in uncovering the beauty in everyone. Everyone is special. Everyone is part of a kaleidoscope. We are all precious and we all must find our own beauty. It's there, underneath the layers, but because we have had so many, many experiences in our life, the seed of light gets covered as a cocoon gets covered.

Many bad things happen too often to us. Many good things also happen, but frequently we don't feel worthy of this. So the seed of light gets completely covered and this keeps going on through years and years and years. Then you finally become an adult and say, "Who am I? What is this all about?

What am I here for?" Then most people begin the huge job of uncovering.

We shall do the job in this book of trying to uncover everyone's beauty. The seed is seeking light; did you know that? We cannot seek light so tightly bound in a cocoon. We are all angels, angels of God. The Creator is drawing close to us all of the time. But it's as if we can't see or feel God sometimes because it's so dark in the cocoon. So we are going to try to open up by many, many experiences.

I would like to say at this time that there is a beautiful way to start opening up. When your soul is in the cocoon state, it is as if a fan is closed very tightly right in your chest. We wish to say that when you open that fan you are receiving total guidance, coming from above, coming from your own self. We are all connected, we are all connected to God, we are all oneself. When we learn to keep the fan open at all times, our guidance is whole, beautiful, pure, and perfect.

Perhaps something would come to you, that you would have a question about. One good way to learn about the fan is to FEEL in your chest a closed fan. As a question comes, does the fan expand or does it stay closed? Is it a "yes," is it a "no"? Yes is a very open beautiful fan. Closed is very tight, doesn't feel good, feels constricted, feels binding. But to start to seek the light, we must be open to be on our journey, and that is our mission. For God wants all of us to be so happy, so in the light and walking with the Creator.

Often ones on earth have gotten far off the track. The fan will be your guiding instrument, as if you are "driving" an airplane, that is our vision. And when you learn expansion and closing and feel it and really FEEL it, life can be so beautiful, so interesting and totally freeing, when you trust that this is so. It is very easy to feel expansion and closing. Closing is when you know it doesn't feel right, that gut feeling that says, "That doesn't feel right. Why did I do it?" And then almost always you suffer the consequences. You say, "I wish I wouldn't have, I wished I would have listened!" But often what happens when we feel it's not right, our head says, "Nope, I'm going to alter that. The head is smarter than my heart-soul area." So what we would like to teach, if possible, to all our wonderful students, is to keep your fan open. The essence of your Creator and angel love and wisdom can only come to you through an open fan in your chest-soul area. You can only receive your own pure truth this way also. Go only with your fan open and when it's closed, retreat because that is not in the light of God.

Nancy

For me to embrace myself means to learn to find the answers to the questions within myself and to trust what I feel and believe to be the best solution. The most profound opportunity to learn this lesson came during my job search. I did not have a job and was at a point financially where it was crucial that I get one. Those moments can be filled with fear and often lead you to spur-of-the-moment decisions. More than one opportunity presented itself to me so I asked Cameron for guidance. He explained that I needed to step back and tune into myself to see how I felt. "Get quiet and listen. Imagine yourself at each different job. How does it feel? Picture a fan inside of you," he said, "Does it feel open and expanded and make you excited to be there, or do you feel closed in? If you feel closed in, don't go with it."

With each job possibility I applied the fan concept. One particular job offered me much less money than my previous job, had a long commute, and did not have a support system behind it to do the work. I sensed my soul was guiding me to that job anyway. At that point, I had to have immense trust in the correctness of that guidance. I took it and realized it was the perfect decision since everything fell into place.

Money appeared from other sources to make up the difference, the commute became an opportunity for musical exploration, and all the support resources I needed just appeared. Later I understood why it was important that I be there. My soul saw the necessity to go there. I realized that all will be taken care of if we follow our soul guidance.

Carole

Cameron started channeling through me at a time when I needed a big dose of self-love and trust. His special name for me is "this one." I always thought that was endearing. It took me well over a year to trust that I was not somehow making his voice up. I did not have a clue where this wisdom was coming from. How could this mostly masculine voice be coming out of my mouth? As Cameron talked, I was also seeing everything in pictures. It seemed like a moving picture in vivid colors. Sometimes the scenes would backtrack to past lives or move forward thirty or forty years. Sometimes I would even see a person passing from this earth. Years would skip by in a millisecond, but it all made sense and didn't seem fast at the time. Somehow, I felt as if I transferred inside the other person's emotions and could feel their feelings. I could feel their hurt, joy, or if they were scared, sad, or peaceful. What was happening? Was I going crazy? Why me? Hadn't I had enough? Why was this happening? Wasn't I already enough of an outcast?

My family was so upset over my undergoing therapy that we drew apart for over two years. I thought we had always been a close family. My sister and I tried to talk a few times on the phone, but fumbling for the proper words was too uncomfortable. We had clearly chosen different paths. So, we bid each other goodbye for a time. Silence was the best my parents and brother could offer me through the many struggles with my childhood memories. That hurt could not have cut any deeper. On many occasions the thought of death by my own hand sounded all too welcome and seemed the only way out of this hell. What stopped me was the feeling that somehow my parents would "get me" when they died.

When the pain became too unbearable, I decided to leagally change my first and middle name so that I could try to disassociate from the hurt little Carole had endured. As Karmen Marie I found new strength. As I moved through my healing and pain, I was able to go back to the courts months later and reclaim my old name. It was so empowering to be able to stand tall and say I wanted the name back that was given to me at birth.

My wonderful, caring husband and children were my pillars of strength and sanity throughout my therapy. I still felt very isolated and longed for my mother, father and siblings, though, to complete my family. Cameron came through at a time when I was wavering. I thought it might be possible to make peace with my family. I could go back, face my family, apologize (for what, I don't know, telling my truth, I guess), and pretend everything was okay. I thought of this often and each time it caused me great dismay. But at least this way I might be able to get my family back. The thought, however, of doing this thrust me into deep darkness. I no longer wanted to pretend that all was okay when it was not. My mask had to stay off. A path of light was calling to me from my angels. The way seemed well defined. Could I trust it? Could I trust myself? Was I making this all up? I put my trust in Cameron. What could I lose at this point?

I tried to lead my life for the next year based on the fan expansion in my chest. I had to remain quiet to visualize the fan. After a few weeks I could just FEEL whether it was open or closed. If it felt partly closed, I would shift gears until the expansion was felt.

Just as we were starting this book, my father died. I had not seen or talked to him in over two years. Days after his passing he "spoke" to me confirming all I needed to know for closure with him. Earth binds us so tightly sometimes that the truth cannot be spoken. He is now free.

I know now the path of light via the fan holds only truth for me. Life can be so freeing when I just listen to myself and feel the expansion. Truth and goodness always follow.

THREE

Allowing the Truth to Be Spoken

Cameron

𝒯ruth tends to wear many masks, many faces to other people, do you know? People mask the truth by saying, "Oh, believe me, I'm telling the truth," when in fact it is not, it is a denial of truth. So we have to be very cautious when we listen to others. We often want to disrupt their train of thought and say, "No, this is not truth." When we talk to ourself or others, monitoring for truth is appropriate.

We want to teach you today, our lovely students, that the path of truth is really your ticket to the light, so to speak. When you are in a fan expansion, as we talked about in the last chapter, you will find that only truth can be spoken, pure truth, not truth with masks, PURE truth. The fan can be your guidance for life. You will find that if you keep your fan open, life can remain very simple, very uncomplicated. When truth comes with many masks on it, life gets VERY complicated and very unsettled and everyone will be searching every place except in the light for truth.

We wish to teach our lovely students that if you could remain with your fan open, truth will come to you. People do not like to hover around others when ONLY truth is spoken. Often we see that if people find that they do not feel good about themselves, they will remain in an untruthful state. This is as far as God can possibly be away from us. It is quite necessary for our wholeness to follow in the Creator's shadow, we do see that.

When we use the word "God," that is our personal word, but you know many people wish for other words and that is proper and good. You can use "Being," you can use "Light," you can use anything that is higher to self that you can rely on. Anything that has strength of love, but not power over, is what you can really depend on. So, if we use the word "God," we do not want anyone to feel uncomfortable. We want you to know that is the way we're speaking in this book. This is a comfortable word for this one (Carole) who I am speaking through. So you can use any word that brings you comfort.

The path of light can serve you for an eternity, it can serve everyone. You can go any place you want with this. You could become what you call the wealthiest person in the world, but true wealth really is being filled with light. We would like to teach our students to trust themselves, to trust the fan, to trust the light. This takes a lot of energy and a lot of self-love. We want to teach you that.

To always be able to feel the expansion in the your chest is so wonderful and good. But it is a problem with trusting that we see those on earth have. They say, "Well, my head does not speak, so how can it be truth?" What we would like to aim for in this chapter, is to try to have your guidance come from your heart-soul area and not from your head.

Heads are wonderful, we want to say that. But often that

is an escape avenue for people when they really do not want to speak the truth. They can get up into their head and mull things over so many times and it comes out and they think to themselves, "Oh, that sounds good and proper." But if it does not come from the heart and soul, it often is not the guidance you are seeking. Sometimes guidance coming from your heart is risky, is it not? If you could continue to trust your feelings and the expansion in your chest, nothing but truth could come to you. You also know that consequences can become very large when you get into your head too much. And you might possibly think you could ignore the big feeling in your heart-soul area.

We wish to tell you the importance of following the path. Goodness will come to you when you do that. You were started as a wonderful, beautiful little seed. And as we explained in the last chapter, many earthly layers are added on to bind your soul. These layers are the consequences and experiences that happen to you on earth. Pretty soon they get so tightly bound in your chest area that you are not on track with the light at all. We would like to open this.

It's sad for us to see how many people are wounded. Many are wounded by others and many are wounded by themselves. How could this happen? How could you wound yourself? When you are in a state of comparing yourself to others and you see yourself as less than they are, your soul binds tighter. Rejoice for who you are. Compare yourself to no one. You know sometimes we see that you on earth are your own harshest critics. Often we see that one wounds others when their hurt is so intense that they think, "I must pass it on to someone else; it would be less on me."

To find your source of light, could you step down from your head and hover in the soul area? Just try it perhaps and see how that would feel. See if the little tiny voice that you hear way down deep in your chest could be correct. Possibly it would be worth giving credence to that little voice, and just see where it takes you.

Maybe you could try it a couple of times when the consequences wouldn't be so big and see what happens. See what the outcome is even though your head would completely flip it over and say, "Oh, that is not true; that is nonsense." Perhaps trying just a few times would be assurance for you that this is truth. This will be one of the harder lessons to do because without following your heart-soul area, nothing of means can be accomplished, you know.

Money is very important to those on earth, we do see that. Money is not important to the soul. The soul wishes for only goodness. I believe that if you put all your energies into the knowledge that you have stored in your heart-soul area, your head will follow. Your soul will be in total "agreeance" that this is truth. This takes a risk to do this. This is uncommon for most people. We do believe from this, that many great things will come. Your life will be more full. We believe what you are all striving for is the light, but often you cannot see the light because things are bound so tightly. Perhaps we shall close this chapter now.

Carole

Cameron made a statement in chapter two that really gave me an unsettled feeling. He said, "People do not like to hover around others when ONLY truth is spoken." I felt sure Nancy and I needed to edit this out; he must have gotten mixed up. But, we had agreed long ago that not one thought of Cameron's would be eliminated or changed, so his statement stayed in. But, his words still gnawed at me. I was truthful, I was sure of that, and I liked to be around those who spoke truth, so what did he mean? I can only apply this to my own life in saying that if people really did share what was AL-WAYS on their mind, or their opinions, or feelings, speaking only in truth, it would cause a lot of stirring and an uncomfortable feeling would come over me. A comfort buffer would seem necessary.

I spoke my truth to my family and immediately became detached from them, almost as if I was on the outside looking in. I did not buffer my truth for them and look where it got me. My truth scared my family away. Cameron was right! Many times going back and smoothing things over with my parents and siblings seemed the only way. Not having a family I could visit or talk to affected so many parts of my life, especially during the holidays! I would go through the process of rejoining them in my mind so often, but each time the fan in my chest stayed so tightly closed that it ached.

I decided I must continue to trust, and trust I did. Following my expanded fan led me to some of the most beautiful souls. I can hardly believe the goodness that has come to me through new-found friends and old friendships which are strengthened. I feel so blessed as my second family surrounds me in light.

Nancy

Before I can allow the truth to be spoken, I have to understand what truth is. Truth gnaws at me. It's something that says, "This doesn't feel right. I see things differently." At those times when I believe differently than what is being spoken around me, I will feel that gnawing inside. Cameron has helped me learn to take notice of those times. "Listen and believe in yourself," he said. "That is your truth speaking."

For so many, many years I discounted my feelings, my truth. "Oh, what do you know," I'd say. "I felt I must be wrong if everyone else thought differently or didn't admit the truth." Now I trust myself and take notice when that gnawing feeling occurs. I realize what my truth is. It may not be how other people see things, but if I follow my belief, then I'm happier and healthier. When I am struggling to identify my truth or what's bothering me I have learned to incorporate the fan exercise. If I feel expanded with what I think I need to say or do, then it's right. If I don't, then, it's wrong. Fear jumps in to complicate things. At times, fear of being judged or hurting others' feelings makes me afraid to speak my truth. The challenge for me is to see fear when it comes and notice how it interferes with the fan and speaking my truth. All along the way I ask God for help.

I met and began to date a very beautiful and spiritual man. The love he radiated drew me to him. My fan was very expanded when I was with him. We shared the same values and interests and enjoyed the same things. We dated for several months.

There was a beautiful depth in the strong feelings I felt we had for each other, but as time progressed, the truth was never spoken.

I decided to speak my truth and express my love for him. What followed was an experience in contradictions. I could see love in his eyes and feel it, but his behavior spoke otherwise. He said he didn't feel it. The beautiful, loving energy that radiated from him to me was the exact opposite of what he was saying.

My belief was that I knew the truth. However, I honor the fact that each of us has our own truth. The painful fact was that I knew my soul did not want me to continue in a situation where the truth as I saw it was not being spoken.

Because my truth was different than his, I felt myself beginning to force my truth on him. It felt pushy and unnatural. Due to this, my fan closed. I couldn't be around him anymore and pretend there wasn't a deep and beautiful relationship between us. Each of us must discover our own feelings without pressure from someone else; I knew that.

Hours were spent with God as I asked for a solution. Time would reveal the truth, I heard, time apart. I ended the relationship. That was one of the most difficult things I've ever done. Though my heartache seemed to last forever, I did begin to feel more at peace with myself. Comfort surrounded me as I realized my love for him would remain within me and that it was necessary to speak to him, regardless of the outcome. Finally, after all these years on earth, I wasn't afraid to speak about how I felt and express my truth. I felt in alignment with my soul.

FOUR

Truth Wears Many Masks

Cameron

*W*e wish at this time to validate that truth wears many masks. We wish for our lovely students to know that truth comes with the word "caution." As little children we are entitled to look at our mothers and fathers as standing only for truth, that is all we know. In some cases you will find many mothers and fathers are perfect, wonderful. They guide their children to full potential.

Often mothers and fathers are not in truth. A small child would ONLY think parents are truthful. They have no other choice. We would almost like to say at this time that a mother would be wearing a mother mask, father wearing the father mask. And somehow a small child gets it in their mind that because they are my parents that means everything is in truth. We wish to say that is not so.

This happens more often than we even like to think. Many children are wounded this way. They say, "I will trust, I will trust." Children often go back to parents who have offended them many times. They feel secure in it for some reason and that is understandable.

In this book we see we cannot help the little ones so much, but what we must do is bring about an awareness for all. This book is really geared for adults. What we think will happen is that adults will become more aware and in the future, their children will too. Adults need to start to understand that sometimes even their mothers and fathers, though held sacred to them, could possibly have been harmful to them. The same can at times be true of people in high, powerful positions and even powerful people in churches. These ones can often hide behind their masks very much. We wish for you to really start looking. If something SEEMS truthful to you, but does not FEEL right in the heart-soul area, it is to be examined further.

We suggest that because someone has high credentials and big dollars, although important to ones on earth, that does not mean truth will always be spoken. Often times that is a coverup. At this time we would not like to lump people together. There certainly ARE truthful people in high power, that is for sure. Just be cautious, be very, very cautious.

We would like to turn the tides of awareness of truth on earth if possible. If there becomes an awareness in the adult, we hope that eventually it will filter down to the small ones.

Often times we see many professions carry a lot of power on earth. We see the individuals in high power are often scared. They started out as a lovely seed, but their experiences and consequences made them so tightly bound in their soul area that they got scared. So they had to get up into their head. They became very brilliant in the mind, but somehow the heart-soul area got lost. It is tightly bound behind so much. Often times we see ones with a lot of power misuse it so much because they are very wounded, not always, but often.

Our caution is to avoid putting those with power on a pedestal and do not believe everything they say. Often we find these ones are just wounded themselves. Somehow, to help themselves feel better, they think they must wound others in the same way. They can wound in so many ways. This brings them more sadness, and so they reach for more power.

Our only purpose in telling you this is to emphasize that "caution" is a big word here. If you follow your own heart-soul area, you would never be, in any way, tricked by this.

We find that ones with great power really would like to strive for the light, but they often don't know how. The power has gotten so big that there are many, many walls to break down. Power and money are so important to them. This brings us a big sadness. On earth, power means truth, some think. Certainly everyone in high power might not be in an untruthful state. We just want you to be more cautious with what people say. Sometimes ones get so awed by another's power that they don't even want to look within that person. They just want to look at their shell and see what it represents to them.

Money has such big power on earth, it can represent so much. People don't think they have to look inside of those with big dollars. Ones with power and money can sometimes be rude to people. They may even slough people off and the one being ignored can say, "Well, that's okay, they have a lot of money." That is a big sadness, especially for the one doing the hurting. It would be a wonderful mission if we could touch some of these people in higher power. That higher power is in their mind and in the minds of others. Everyone is absolutely the same.

JOURNEY TO YOUR SOUL

We all start out as the same beautiful seed of light made by God. Only experiences push some up onto the pedestal very very fast. Often times they don't even know what hit them and they're just on this pedestal and they say, "What happened?" Sometimes they might even forget their manners. We would like to bless those people especially. They have asked for a very hard mission in order to learn much. People look up to them. Power often scares people. They say, "I don't know how I got here; I don't have all the answers like others think I do. What can I do?" So they often put a big shield tightly around them to keep people away.

We see people with extremely high power almost have to have guards around them to keep others away from them. That is sad. Their soul is searching for so much more. But how do they start to unravel, it's too big a job. Too much face for them to lose really.

We would be so pleased now to be able to reach everyone. In our eyes everyone is exactly the same, everyone is perfect. Everyone has their own power right inside of them. We would hope that everyone reading this book can find their own power. Only then will everyone be on the same level, no one higher than anyone else. That is our mission.

The next time you watch a movie star on TV, just know that they have been given a fake power without even knowing it. This happens often when people watch them on TV or the big screen. Perhaps you can think to yourself, this is not only someone on the big screen, this is also a beautiful soul of God. And could you possibly think that you are the same as them. They are headed for the same path of light as you.

It does people no good to be given special reverence, I want to tell you that, it does their soul harm really. No one wants to be treated differently. If anyone ever thinks they deserve to be treated very highly, that is coming from their mind.

Their heart-soul area does not want that. Do a kindness next time, treat them as you. You might get a little flicker of light from their beautiful soul.

We want to bless everyone at this point who is in a very high position or who has a very high name on earth. They have asked for a very difficult mission. They wish for this to teach them much. Please, next time you do get in a situation where you are around these ones, bless them heavily on their path.

Carole

For me, the title of the third chapter, "Truth Wears Many Masks" hits home. I had my father on a pedestal from infancy on, probably not unlike a lot of little girls. I thought he was the best, the smartest, the kindest. I thought he would protect and take care of me always. He also wanted me to keep many secrets. That made me feel special, just between Daddy and me and no one else. I thought I must really be precious to him if we could not share our times with anyone, they were only for us. I guess I could say his "father mask" made me believe what he was doing was okay because I often heard, "Honor thy father." I just figured this is what fathers were all about.

I got the idea mommies also wanted you to keep secrets. Mommy taught me well to keep my feelings, thoughts, and voice to myself. So, with her confirming this, I just thought this must be what family life was all about. You keep happenings to yourself.

My way of handling what was happening was to forget most of the hurtful occurrences. Some of the memories have been with me forever. My mind would usually dredge up part of a scene when I was feeling low about myself, almost as if to add insult to injury. But, as usual I kept my thoughts to myself.

_____

When the rest of my memories came bubbling up full bore, I was sure my mother and father would come to my aid and immediately help me through this crisis. They had always been there before when I needed them, so I was sure they would be there again. After all, they are my parents and this was by far the most painful thing I had ever been through! I thought they would say that they made a terrible mistake long ago and that they were hoping I wouldn't remember. But now that I have, they would want to know how they could help me and make it easier. I wanted them to say that my memories were correct and that I was not stupid afterall. I wanted them to say they were sorry, so very sorry and to please forgive them. At that point I really needed to hear that they were remorseful. That seemed very important to me then. The word "sorry" would have been so healing for me. It seemed my forgiving them would come a lot easier if they had spoken their truth. Their silence amazed me.

Through the family grapevine I heard they now deemed me mentally ill. What were they talking about! Don't they remember? I guess you really *don't* tell family secrets. Their silence was clear, it spoke volumes. I now know the secrets were not an okay thing, but a sad happening that was occurring inside the confines of this family. I had been tricked. How could they? I trusted them. I felt betrayed!

I still wonder why I was so trusting as a child. Was I stupid like my Dad said or was it just that my circumstances were such that I had to trust them for my survival? Yes, the mother-father mask meant truth to me. How would any tiny child know the difference? How sad it is to be betrayed by your own parents, the ones you entrusted your security and life with.

Nancy

Once I put someone on a very high pedestal. I'd never known anyone with so much love to give to the world. People who knew him said he had a glow about him. Some said he radiated love unconditionally to everyone and everything around him. I could imagine what Jesus was like after having known Tom Oddo, a young Catholic priest who was president of the University of Portland. I felt blessed to be able to know him while working at United Way. He was the volunteer chairman of a committee I was in charge of. We worked along side each other for three years.

Most people around him were in awe of him. He was deeply revered. I expected him to know everything and I sensed the divinity and Godliness within him. He filled the university and community with his love, energy, and brought abundance wherever he went.

Then suddenly he was gone. The beacon of light was extinguished. He was killed tragically in a freak automobile accident. The gaping hole in our world was enormous. How could such a beautiful spiritual being be ripped from us? The impact of his life was amplified by his death.

Years went by and many of us could not sort through our grief, nor understand. Then a few months ago, I began to understand.

It had been several years since I had thought of him and the lessons he taught me. During that time I had healed from my childhood, evolved in my awareness and consciousness, and experienced a spiritual awakening. My extensive journaling helped me to slowly open to another dimension of consciousness. Guidance and love from my angels poured into me. I had even been able to connect with Cameron through my writing and with that my abilities increased over time. There was tremendous love and wisdom coming through, but I had to develop and evolve before I could hear it. My listening deepened.

Suddenly, one day out of the blue, Tom came through to me while I was writing. I was stunned. It was amazing to me how I instantly knew it was him. I had not thought of him nor asked for his guidance; however, beyond a doubt I understood it to be him. His radiant energy engulfed me. He wanted to talk to me. In large, scrawling letters that flowed and flowed, I began to write his words.

Tom

I had grown weary of the expectations. I felt as if I had lost myself in my service to others. My love of God grew immensely as I followed my spiritual path. A deepening occured within me and with it gratitude for the love I received from God. As I deepened spiritually, a schism began to develop between my earthly side and my spiritual side. I felt less and less connected to the people around me and to my deeper self. My soul hungered for the opportunity to be whole, but my chosen faith and path did not allow an integration of both sides of me. This saddened me and caused pain as my life progressed. I did not feel comfortable when people worshipped me.

We are all equal in God's eyes. I began to want to express my human side, to feel whole, to be in balance. I believe this is what my Lord intended for me, to be in balance.

Humans at times create an artificial lifestyle that prevent its spiritual leaders from being human and whole. I felt the conflict and the pressure to be perfect and all knowing. I became lonely. I wanted more opportunities to express my human side. But for me they were not available.

Nancy

Pages were now filled with his thoughts, feelings and beliefs. I was humbled by his presence and could still feel the beauty of this spiritual being. Only this time I was seeing a different side, and began to understand.

I understood that he liked people to call him Tom. He wanted to be a person as well as a man of God. He did not feel comfortable being idolized and worshiped. He grew to be unhappy and wanted to be free.

My minister once said, "Let us remember that as spiritual and beautiful as Jesus was, he also had feelings and was a real person. He too had moments of fear and sadness." Remembering that, I became very sad as I realized Tom's truth.

He wanted to experience all parts of himself and feel he was balanced. God also wanted this for him. His position did not allow that, nor would the people allow for that, they expected godliness from him all of the time. Tom wanted people to realize that he very much was everything he appeared to be spiritually, but he was also a man. The religious trappings became a mask that covered his human side.

Why do humans worship other people? In some cases, we even give up our own beliefs to follow others and what they believe. Soon we lose ourselves in the process. This is an unkindness, both to ourselves and to them. We can learn from these people, which is why they're here. They are not better than we are. I see how unfair we are to people when we put them on pedestals, how difficult it is for them and that we do it because we lack self-love.

Sometimes the mask becomes the position, the money, the stardom. It covers the real person. Some of these people have found their souls and speak the truth, some have not and are hiding behind their masks. All masks prevent us from living in truth and realizing we are all the same. We all are seeking peace and love within ourselves. The paths take different turns, but all are seeking God and light.

Tom helped me understand that living in balance is God's intention. I see how unfair we can be to people by worshiping them and how much pain and imbalance this can create for them. We seek truth from these people when in reality, truth only comes from ourselves and God.

Cameron is teaching me to find my own truth. Truly, if I trust what my instincts (heart-soul area) are saying and follow those, I know my life will be filled with love, peace, and abundance.

FIVE

Cameron

*O*ftentimes people of great power are put on pedestals by others. They are revered. Sometimes we think that their path is the one to be followed, something to be fashioned by. The shirt-tailers, we shall call them, believe that if they walk in the path of such a one they will add a greatness to themselves, and will gain power. This is a fake power, it is not a real power. It is a path only for that person, and no one else. We do little service to these people to put them at a height beyond us. That is not what their soul wishes, that's only what their head may wish.

And we would like to say at this time to our lovely students, please don't ever put anyone higher or lower than another person. We are all perfect seeds of God. We're all exactly and completely the same. What we're doing to the ones we put on a pedestal is such a grave disservice to their soul. We need to have you understand that so heavily today.

It seems as if the earth likes to choose people just by coincidence. Sometimes they go up the ladder of success very quickly, or they win, say, even the lottery. They win and they become more important to others, and then they are made into someone that they are really not. What a disservice to these people. Oftentimes we think if we rub elbows with people with lots of money that we may be the same in wealth and knowledge and more. That is only from the head. Our heads are doing that kind of leading, not our souls. What we need to do for these precious people is bless them heavily as they go on their path. We do bless them so heavily. But do not follow.

Don't ever take anyone's path and say, "Well, I will follow, that will be good for me. That will bring me stardom, make me a big name, and lots of money." Your head is leading you, that is for sure, when you think this way. That is such an unkindness for both of you. Your soul doesn't want that. Your soul has its own path.

Be very wary of anyone who wishes to be your leader and then says, "Follow me, if you hang around me I will give you a feeling that you're more powerful." If you stick around them, they say, you will have a greatness. They say they have all the answers. Be wary of this. How can that be? How can anyone be better than anyone else? We all start out the same beautiful seed of light. God made us all. He didn't make anyone more precious than anyone else. We're all the same preciousness. Who is it that can do this? Only us, only we can put others on a pedestal.

When we are bound tightly in the heart-soul area for some reason we can't see or feel the light calling to us. We often don't feel good about ourselves, so we start looking around us to find a shirt-tail to tag onto and say, "With that person I will be great. I will follow in his footsteps." What happens when you do this is that the other person thinks they have so much glory. That is all in their head and in yours, of course. That's not kind to them, and is such a "misservice" to both of you. What it does to you is take you COMPLETELY off your path. And then you start getting bound heavily in the chest-soul area.

What we would like to teach you lovely ones today is to try to search for your own path. Just because people are on a pedestal, people often say, "Well, they have it all, they have all the answers." Sometimes your mind makes a conclusion that when they are on a pedestal they are somehow holier, you know.

We often do that with priests and people in churches in high places. What a "misservice" to do to these ones. They are there to serve God. They are not really there in a way to lose themselves, but oftentimes this is what happens to these ones. They've lost themselves in the search for God; really that is what's happening. People grab and take and call them special names, and these souls don't like this at all. This draws too much from them. Oftentimes we see that these ones have to leave earth early. They can't take this pressure. They are just the same as anyone else. No one is different, no one is different at all. If we could be able to get everyone on the same level, we would rejoice! It would be a wonderful goal to have this happen in say, the next 200 years in earth time. Don't ever look down on someone or up at someone, just know they are equal.

This unequality happens often in the business place. There always has to be someone that is "head of" and then all the little worker bees underneath. That's the way they do it. And the person that's "head of" has so much power. That brings us a sadness because they think they are more powerful, but they are not. Their soul is so lost, and they get so confused.

It may be a surprise to you lovely ones, but the ones in

higher power are often really the loneliest. It appears they have lots of friends and everyone is vying for their attention, but they are so often lonely inside. We can even see this in some of the very high name actors-actresses, big screen people. We see people, big screen names, are often so lonely. Their face is splashed all over and almost everyone seems to think they must be more special than other people. They are so, so revered by many people. Ones say, "Oh, if I could be like them, I would be okay." Well, that is so sad for us to hear because those are often the loneliest people. Most of the time they are searching the hardest.

Oftentimes we see that people of very, very little means are the ones who are really more connected into themselves. Oftentimes what we want to say is that the homeless people really are quite in tune with themselves. They only have themselves to go to and are really at one with God; they have no one else. They have not become bound quite so tightly, no one is vying to be in their position.

And so what we would like to say to all of our lovely people today is that when you come in the presence of our lovely ones who have a big name, I want you to understand their path, it's very difficult. Something has pushed them up the ladder before they even know what happened to them, and their mission is very much a struggle for them.

I would like to say that you can do a big, big kindness by trying to always see others as you, never different, *never different*, never higher, never lower. Please smile at a homeless person, smile at someone on the street. Look right into their eyes. You will see a beautiful soul in someone who is homeless. Someone who is dirty, who is tattered and torn is just as precious as you, just as precious as the million-billionaire, just as precious, no different whatsoever.

You all have the same beautiful souls! If you could start

looking INTO people, into their eyes and look beyond what they represent to you, you would see their soul. We believe you will have a lot of soul connections and that is so important for living life to its fullest, being connected is so necessary. It is often very difficult to become connected to people you see on the big screen, because all you see is their outer shell and what they represent to you. In trying to view anothers soul you may not get past their shell. Could you possibly look into their eyes and try to see their soul?

In the next chapter we would like so much to go into the soul connection with people. But to be able to do that and to understand the feeling, would it be possible when you look at someone next time, to look deep into their eyes? Look beyond their eyes and see a beautiful soul shining, and make a special attempt to look into people that you NORMALLY shy away from. This is mostly because what they represent for you is not proper you think. If you could try that for awhile, you would find some amazing things would happen. We'll bless all of you today and the next chapter will be coming very soon.

Carole

For so many years of my life I often had my father and mother on a pedestal. When they came crashing down right before my eyes, I felt so exposed, so scared. It seemed there was no one that I could look to for guidance and security, or so I thought. I now had to find my own way. When I knew that my parents were incapable of being any foundation for me, where could I go? I remember being told frequently as a child that I was stupid. Soon, even I came to believe it was true. This message was sent loud and clear in words and through body language. I couldn't even take off that extra twenty pounds that seemed to plague me my adult life. Will I always be a failure? Where will I get my answers? Who can I lean on?

My parents included me as part of the family even with my meager smarts. What now? Did I even have a path waiting for me? It seemed unlikely to me, already in my late forties, that I could find it now. How could I ever make a dent in the world? I could never venture out and take a risk because my dad just might be right. How could I ever expose myself to something new? What if I failed? How long could I pretend I'm just as smart as others, if perhaps I'm not?

When Cameron started channeling through me, Nancy and I kept it to ourselves. I was much more fearful than she that I would be judged as strange or weird. I wondered if I was losing my mind because I was hearing voices or even, maybe, that gnawing word "stupid." It also seemed embarrassing to me. After all, my whole life had already been turned upside down with therapy. How much could my friends and family hear without tiring of my ever-changing life? Cameron became a well-kept secret. One day a friend and I were in deep conversation when I heard Cameron say, "Tell her about me." I hesitated, but after thinking it over, I felt comfortable enough to share my secret with this spiritual woman.

The time was right. She was mourning the recent loss of her sibling, and I hoped Cameron could offer her some comfort. Cameron did indeed come through after she showed an interest in hearing him. I was amazed to find Cameron was able to relay facts as well as comfort from her deceased sibling. Cameron gave my friend the closure she needed in knowing that her sibling was now okay, safe, and so happy to be freed of earth's bondage.

Cameron said one of his missions now is to be my protector due to the fact that I am quite open to the spirits. He says some who wish to speak through me are not for my highest good. He adds, however, that he will relay messages from others on his side to loved ones here through me.

Many times since then I have heard Cameron say, "Tell him or her about me." I now trust that voice to know that this person will be accepting of Cameron and that a message of paramount healing will come through. Cameron has never failed on this for anyone. I have seen some amazing healing and closure for people from hearing Cameron's words. This is so profound to watch. It feels so right to me now. I feel so very blessed.

Cameron tells us he will be around for my healing, and the healing of others, and to channel this book. And then, he will be gone, except for an occasional visit. His mission, he says, in this book is only to set the pillars down and do the spiritual groundwork. Then a higher spirit in teaching will continue where he left off. I can already feel her presence.

I find that when Cameron does so much healing using my voice, people sometimes think I might have their answers even when I'm not channeling him. Their answers are within them. I have only been given the gift of being open to the angels. We all can be open if we really choose. People's gifts come in so many forms. I now find Cameron does hover close for many of my conversations and often drops tidbits of his wisdom into my head at appropriate times. I will always continue to credit him in the eyes of others when I choose to use his words. We can always find the answers to all our questions in our soul area. We can tap into them at will, just by listening to that little voice.

Now I see how such a gift as mine can go to your head and might make you think you do have other people's answers. You may even consider youself to have extra wisdom due to this ability. Unfortunately this gift can lead you to being put on a pedestal, by yourself or others. For me, that would be frightening and make me feel separate. The pedestal position is not one that is comfortable for me. It took me so long to find my path of light that to step off it for some fake glory is unthinkable. The light is leading me in the opposite direction.

Tom

I wanted to know many people around me. I wished to spend time with friends and be able to relax. However, so many respected my position that they froze when they were around me. I had only a few very close friends who were able to be themselves with me. It was as if I made others uncomfortable when I was being myself. I stopped being myself because of the discomfort it caused others. They expected a god, not a man. I understood that and it saddened me, for I was a man.

Few people were brave enough to ask how I was. What was I worried about? Few expected me to worry or to have feelings. Where was the honesty and understanding that comes from sharing with friends for me? It seemed few could relate to where I was in my growth. People seemed awkward in their conversations with me. The fact that I was causing them to feel uncomfortable distressed me deeply. I felt so much love, and wanted to share it with others. My position only allowed for a relationship like that with God.

That caused me great pain. God brought people into my life to help me grow and be my teachers. Earthly rules forbid me from accepting God's gifts.

I am speaking through my friend, Nancy, because she is not afraid. She listens and cares in return. I want her to carry my message to earth. It is wrong to prevent our spiritual leaders from experiencing all parts of themselves. It causes pain and so much closing in their souls. In effect, instead of assisting in the spiritual growth of these children of God, it stifles their love of self and the natural evolution of the soul. God intended all parts of us to be considered beautiful, which we are. The beauty I am experiencing now is beyond words.

Here I am free. I wasn't free on earth. What a sad thing to do to anyone, encase them in a box and then elevate them onto a pedestal.

My mission on earth was complete. It continues now with Nancy and this book. There must be a change on earth so that humans may evolve to another level of consciousness and love. Each soul must discover truth and balance for itself. This cannot be dictated by someone else. It creates the death of a soul. As I began to feel the death of my soul I asked God to allow me to be free to express all parts of me. He answered my prayer. He took me.

He also had a plan for me to send a message back to earth through my precious friend, Nancy. There will be a far greater impact through this book than I could ever have had in my life. I accepted this mission, and am humbled by God's love for me.

SIX

Soul Bonding Is Possible

Cameron

*B*onding with one's soul is the ultimate task we wish to undertake today for our lovely students. We find you strive for this often in your life and bonding really is the essence of living. Bonding with one's soul is quite easy, you know, for the soul can be seen beyond the eyes. If you look INTO the eyes, the soul can be seen. It's as if a light is shining, as if in the fog. If you were to look on an ocean and look way far into the distance, you might somehow see a light out there from a ship. So, you have to look very, very deeply into someone's eyes. Almost go beyond their eyes to see a beautiful soul shining.

Our purpose today for you lovely people is to teach you that this is available to you at any time. And when you can soul bond with someone, there becomes a connection that nothing can sever. We wish you to be able to look beyond their mouth, and beyond their shell when you talk to others.

And we wish for you to be able to look WAY DEEP into their eyes and then you will get a soul connection with them. You could almost feel the sensation shoot down into your soul area, and down into your stomach area. It is almost like a shooting wave of, what shall we say, almost an energy feeling that you will feel way deep down in there.

To be able to do this is such a gift, and it can be done by all. You will find when you do this, that in one way we are all connected as one. Everyone is absolutely no different at all. Only the shells of people are different, really, and their experiences make them different. But we really are all the same, one hundred percent the same. When we can start realizing this, we can break away, break away from the shells we are in and expose ourselves for who we are. Because we are all the same, there is nothing to hide.

The next time you look into someone's eyes, try not to be embarrassed by staring just an instant longer and just getting that one better look. Oftentimes we see ones have a hard time looking people in the eyes. It kind of brings a blush to them. It brings an embarrassment to them. Why is that? Do you understand? We often find what really happens is that when people look deep into our eyes somehow we think that they can see what we have or haven't achieved or what we are not too proud of, or we feel exposed. We almost feel naked sometimes. We don't like that feeling.

Perhaps a good way to start this would be with a friend that you feel very comfortable with who would think this might be a fun experiment. Look into their eyes, DEEP into their eyes and allow yourself to do this for several minutes. Just kind of LOSE yourself in those beautiful, shining eyes; almost like marbles, aren't they, they're lovely. Look beyond them, think of nothing around you. See how deep you can look into their eyes and just hunt for that shining light. When you find the light, there will come a bonding. The two of you will bond and become one. What a beautiful gift we could give to each other if we would allow this to happen.

Often we find that when people walk down streets or in crowds with people they don't know, their eyes look down to the pavement. They do not wish to look into peoples'eyes. They don't want to soul connect. They don't even know that bonding is what would be happening if they looked into another's eyes. They believe that something about them might be shameful, so they wish not to be exposed. They also think if they look straight into someone's eyes those people may want something that they really don't want to give. We don't really know, there are lots of reasons why people don't like to look at each other. We oftentimes find that when people are not in truth, they will not look anyone in the eyes. Their eyes will dart around to many places. We're sad about that because that's when you're the furthest away from soul connection, you're so far away from connection to anyone. That is not your mission on earth, your mission is to be connected to and with each other.

We see you are striving to find your own beauty, your own destiny, and to find that you are all the same. When we do not look into people's eyes, we find ourselves isolated from them, disconnected from them. Since we are all part of God, in a way you are really disconnected from God.

After you have practiced this lesson, if you dare, with a friend, quite amazing things will happen. You will want to soul bond and be around them often. You'll feel so connected, as if you've never felt connected before. Once you've learned this lesson well and you are able to put down your guard just for a minute and start looking into the eyes of strangers, you will find you're connecting right and left with people. Sometimes because you're connecting, you might think they have more interest in you possibly than before, so in the next chapter we give you a bit of caution about this. Do not over emphasize looking into eyes. It does not have to come with a duty attached to it. It only has to be for a connection of the soul and then that's it. It is just for a second and it's gone, and you have reconnected with that one. Then you can go on and see other strangers and you both will be okay. It does not mean that you'll need to walk a path with everyone whose eyes you look deep into on the street.

This could come with caution when looking deep into ones eyes. We just want to say there are always, always two sides to something. We don't want to put any fear in. That is NOT the idea to put any fear in at all. But, as always, when you are in a situation, there's always two sides. If there are not two sides, it would not be proper. That will be explained later in other chapters. But, just know for now that everything has two sides to it, two meanings to it. This takes a lot of nerve, you know, to be able to look right square in the eye of someone because they may pull back and think, well, what does this person want from me? What is it? What are they seeing? They may not like it too much. But you know if you get to that point that you can look deep into their eyes, and in a way having them do the same to you, wonderful things will happen for both of you. And that is really our mission.

We would love to find a unity in this world. It has to start someplace, and we must start with an eye connection because that's where the soul can be seen. If we do not soul connect, people will be disconnected and disjointed from themselves and others in every facet of living. Our mission is to get you all on a path to the light of God. This is very simple, but it must start small and grow. Pretty soon it will become like dominos. And it will spread, it will spread throughout the world. That would be such a joy to us here.

Todays lesson has been a big one. It is so wonderful and it brings you such a good feeling when you can find someone's soul. Bless all of you and goodbye.

Nancy

When people look deeply into my eyes, I become afraid. I look away, and am not comfortable. Recently, I have asked myself why this is so?

I prayed to God to help me understand what this was telling me about myself. My answer was that I was afraid of my own feelings when people looked at me, especially if I saw love in their eyes. My reaction didn't seem to be one of guilt or shame, it seemed that I was afraid of what I might feel.

I had learned as a child not to feel. Whenever I expressed my deepest feelings, I remember being hurt in some way. As I experienced soul connections with people these past several weeks, instead of turning away, I stayed with it and allowed myself to feel those feelings. I came home and cried to the depth of my soul. I felt something would happen to me if I let myself feel these deep friendships. Would I be hurt? Remembering how I felt as a child, I cried some more.

An amazing thing happened, I began to heal. It was such a relief. I was not as afraid as I used to be. Now I understand how beautiful this all is. It's about healing our wounds and allowing ourselves to love and be loved by other people. God is love. The more I love, the closer I feel to God.

Tom

My soul wanted to connect with those around me. I would look into people's eyes wanting to share my love. What I witnessed was a great deal of shame. People would look down and I often wondered if it was me, my priest's collar, or what? Perhaps it was all of it. This made me sad as I saw this happen over and over again.

Only on rare occasions did I connect with someone on a deeper level. Nancy was one of those people. I would look into her eyes and the feeling went deep into my soul. However, I knew I could not develop the friendship. She was married and I was a priest. The taboos prevented it. The pain I felt from not being able to develop that friendship was enormous. My soul desired the opportunity to grow. God gives us friendships so that we learn to feel. I now know that the more I feel, the closer I am to God and the wholeness I seek. I began to feel deeply for Nancy.

My life had been so programmed that it did not allow time to feel. I began to feel alive and at the same time confined. My soul felt a conflict between wanting to open up, feel and move closer to God, and not being allowed to. I understood the impossibility of my situation. The spirit of my soul began to die. I felt it and could not find a solution. On earth I did not understand what was happening to my soul. I do now.

When the spirit of a soul begins to die, we begin the slow and painful journey to the death of our entire being. I slowly lost my joy for everything I was doing. I desperately tried to cover this all up and pretend things were as they used to be. I was not being true to myself and what my soul wanted for me. God wanted me to not be afraid to feel and express my feelings. Now I understand that a deep friendship with Nancy on earth was not part of God's plan. The plan was for me to begin to open up and learn how to feel as I witnessed her sweetness and the love she showed to all around her. She touched me with the love she radiated.

I understand, finally. Soul connections, however brief, are the direct pathway to God. If we allow ourselves soul connections, we allow ourselves to feel the beautiful love from these moments. Each time we become more complete and move one step closer to our precious Lord.

Carole

Eye contact has always been a problem for me. A few times over the years people have actually said to me, "What's wrong with your eyes?" or "Why are you looking at my chest?" Sometimes I noticed people glance down at themselves to see what I was looking at. When this happened, I felt terrible. I had no idea I was doing this until they reacted to my wandering eyes. I was aware, though, that looking directly into someone's eyes brought me great mental discomfort. I didn't know why, it just did.

Near the end of my therapy it was discovered that I started this eye habit before I was two years old. It had become such a part of me that I was totally unaware I was doing it. Small children read body language, especially since words don't have much meaning yet. My habit developed as a method of understanding what situation I was in with my father and others. By looking at their hands I was able to read what was coming. It was really my own safety check.

As I became aware of this habit through therapy, I noticed I did this frequently with strangers, especially men. Sometimes I even did this with friends. This happened especially when I had gone off my self-prescribed diet. I felt they could see my self-disgust with another failed attempt at weight loss.

My therapist suggested that whenever I make eye contact and my eyes feel like they want to drop down, to say to myself, "I am safe now." This helped me so much. Often it takes great strength to keep my eyes up, even now that I'm aware that I do this. It seems so natural for me to drop them. I have to be conscious of where my eyes are or they will drop, simply out of habit.

A few times over the past years I have felt safe enough to let myself look into and beyond someone's eyes. The feeling was always positive. However, I just shrugged it off thinking that I might have known this person from my past. It was also curious to me, that somehow in that instant of eye contact, I felt somewhat bonded to them and always remembered the experience. I would bring up that remembrance when I was feeling good about myself. This had only happened a few times in my life up until now.

Cameron has suggested in this chapter that we start our soul bonding, via eyes, with a willing friend. Nancy and I decided to try this. We looked into each others eyes. Then I looked beyond her eyes. I was sure I saw a distant light there. Had a lamp made those tiny yellow spots? No, it was daytime and no lights were on in the house. I did not feel a surge of energy between us, nor did she. I felt sure it was because we had soul bonded long ago. We had such fun doing this that we got the giggles. We decided to practice this on others. I wanted to see if I would get that surge in bonding with a stranger for the first time.

Every place I went during next week or so, I tried looking directly into people's eyes, then deeper for just a millisecond longer. I noticed this seemed uncomfortable for a lot of people. Many would shy away, but a few did allow me a glance.

When I was able to greet someone's eyes in depth, amazing things happened. I felt a surge of energy and bonding with this person. The surge traveled from my chest to my stomach. It seemed as if we had to sneak one last peek at each other to see what was manifesting.

I also have been practicing by watching people on TV. I can stare longer that way without embarrassment. It is easy if they are close up and looking directly into the camera. It was absolutely amazing that I felt the same surge of energy rush inside me. Their eyes became alive right through the TV. At that instant I felt such a kinship to them and felt so equal even though the screen had a way of making them seem more important. This adventure of eye contact is so freeing and healing.

SEVEN

Bonding In the Eyes Comes with Caution

Cameron

We wish to speak today to our lovely students about the possibility that when you are able to look into someone's lovely eyes for just half a second longer, that a reverence will be reached between the two of you. And we wish to tell you at this time that it does not come with any sort of duty attached to it. It does not come with any sort of necessity to do something with this person. It does not come with a bonding other than a soul bonding. We wish to tell you today that when you do look deep into each other's eyes so much can be seen. So much can be seen of the past of people. You can see their hardships, you can see so much, if you really, really get in tune with it. But often times when you connect with someone they may feel, "Well, what have I done? Why have I deserved such a stare? What is it?" People become a little cautious and they almost think you want to take something from them that's theirs. And that is not so.

We wish to tell you that we believe when you have made a soul connection with some lovely ones who have allowed it, you could leave it at that. If you could leave it at the wonderful connection and feel blessed for that instant that you two have bonded, that would be our wish.

We notice that what happens often-times is people use eyes, you know, to get their way. But when people lie to you, they want to look away, they do not want to make eye contact with you. Contrary to this is when people look into one's eyes as if to get power over others, as to intimidate them. We find this often with parents or olders to young children as sort of an intimidation tactic. We find the eyes can be used in many ways. Most ways are glorious, but some people have devised a system where they can have great power over others by looking deep, deep into their eyes to take control of them. The recipient of this becomes almost as a puppet to them. This is where our caution comes in today.

Just because someone looks into your eyes and makes a bonding, or if they look in your eyes for a special purpose for THEM, do not be party to it. You do not need to reciprocate in any way. Do it in an instant flash and go on to the next. We cannot in anyway caution children about an older's desire to look into their eyes and take advantage of them. This is a problem we see on earth. There is really no way to warn these small ones. We are speaking to adults today. And we do believe as generations go along, as the adults learn this, they will pass this on to their children. We hope they will say, "Be cautious of ones who look you in the eye, only cautious IF they have a devious deed behind it." We often think we need to glance at someone in a way of honoring them, and that is true, that is proper. But, if their look to you becomes one of not FEELING right in your chest-soul area, look away. Say "No, you will not take part of me with you. You will not, you will not overtake me with the power of your eyes."

We often see small ones become so intimidated, as if like a puppy they follow those who have drawn them in by an eye contact. This brings us great grief. This is where there is confusion. The eyes can be used for perfection, and they can be used for the opposite. Be a little wary of this when you look into someone's eyes. We do think in times to come you will be able to recognize this. You will be able to see a soul. Sometimes you might see a frightening intensity in someone's eyes. It's just that in some people who have a desired purpose for themselves, you can't see the soul of them. It's bound so tightly. Their eyes have almost closed behind to the window to the soul. Their devious purposes have done this really. We do not want to scare or put any fear into anyone. We just want you to be cautious about this. We are not at all, in any way saying you will not see a soul in everyone.

Soul bonding is a beautiful thing to do, we hope you've been able to practice this a little bit. But just because you have soul bonded does not mean you have a duty to this one or they have a duty to you, it's not that at all. We hope this is understood. You know the problem we see on earth is that people no longer look into one's eyes, or beyond one's eyes. It's almost a big fear. They think that something is expected of them or vice versa.

We wish, at this time, to especially bless the ones who when you look into their eyes, no soul can be seen. These ones would do something that would be only for their own concern, only for their own greatness. We will bless those ones. They need to find the path of light so their soul can show through the window. Please let's all bless them and put them in our care, for one day you will look into their eyes and the window will be open. You will see their soul. We will delight in that, if that were to happen.

If you were to look in one's eyes who are say homeless, maybe someone who you wouldn't want particular contact with or someone on the street who has a can in front of them and says, "Please give me money. I have no job. I have no home," and if you look deep into their eyes, you will see a beautiful soul. We could almost guarantee it. You will bond with them in such a way, it will be so beautiful, it will be so lovely for you to see that. You do not need to feel so sorry for these ones. They have chosen this path, we do know that. We do know that for them to sit on the street corner seems like a challenge to you, but, in fact, it is not a challenge. This is something they have chosen. We have blessed them highly for that mission of theirs. You can learn a lot from these ones, you know. Next time you are in a position to see these ones, perhaps you can look into their eyes and beyond them and you would be absolutely amazed at the shining you will see.

We do not believe they will shun you either, as you might think. You will be very surprised. Oftentimes we see their souls are not bound quite so tightly. They have asked for a hard mission and they ARE doing it well.

We hope today we did not put any kind of fear into you. That is not at ALL what we wish to get across, but we want to say that eyes can be used for so much. The eyes are beautiful windows to the soul. Please next time, when you look into someone's eyes and you can't really see their soul or can't see anything except hurt, bless them especially, because they need it, they need to have that window open and you can help do that, you know.

I think we shall close today, and we do not want to put out too much caution with the eyes, but just an AWARENESS, only an awareness of what happens when you look into others eyes. Bless all of you. Goodbye.

Nancy

At times when I look into people's eyes, I realize that they do not love themselves, and their intentions are not always in my best interest. Opportunities to look deeply into people's eyes have fascinated me recently. It's hard to stay with it as long as I'd like to for my own healing, but I know that if I feel fear or discomfort, this is telling me something about myself as well as something about them. My desire to find out more has led me on. I decided to replay looking into their eyes after I came home, role-playing, if you will. This has caused tremendous healing for me and insight into them, particularly if it was someone I already knew.

My recent relationships have led me to believe that I have been afraid to open up to those I love. I am more open than ever before, but I sense some remaining fears. My goal is to be able to share love free of fear.

My past was still getting in the way. I began to believe that my father was still holding me hostage. So I decided to close my eyes and go back in time in my mind and imagine myself as a child again. I looked into my father's eyes and stayed there. That was very, very hard for me to do. An excruciatingly deep pain surfaced and I felt sick to my stomach. Somewhere a strength came from deep within me and I shifted from pain to understanding and love.

So often we are presented with opportunities like this to heal, but we're scared and back away. We don't want to face it. Oh, to know that we will be okay! Memories make us feel pain, but they don't kill us. We heal. I trusted that, in spite of the pain, this was necessary for my healing. My angel Tom was holding me, I could feel him, and I asked God to help me.

I looked! What scared me was that I knew that my father's eyes always told me what was going to happen. No wonder I had been afraid to look at people's eyes; it was because of what I thought might happen to me.

Memories came that I could both see and feel. What happened to me became clear and the anguish I felt went to the depth of my soul. "God, please walk me into this," I prayed. My determination to face it, feel the pain and be rid of this was all consuming. It's in there festering, always. We wonder why our relationships fail, why we have family difficulties, work difficulties, or health problems. It's within us. I believe we have wounds festering within us and this causes pain in our lives now. My gaze stayed with my father and I saw more. As I cried with rage, I felt my angel pouring love into me. My request was to see and feel it all.

Pretty soon I saw a little boy, he was my father. He had been horribly hurt by his mother. She was cruel to him. My soul could feel the deep pain within the little boy as I heard him say he was sorry to me. Then he walked away. We all have a hurt little boy or girl within us that is crying and wants to heal.

After that I became bathed in light with the people I love. My father was on the outside and couldn't get in. Immense love was radiated to me by those I love. My father wasn't there anymore. A realization came to me that I could give and receive love and not be afraid. I cried myself to sleep with relief.

The next morning I awoke and felt different, I was different! Repeating this exercise with people whose gaze I didn't trust and with those I do, has taught me to see a difference between those people who love me and want to give love and those who are wounded and can't give me love. I'm grateful that I'm able to recognize the difference and trust my knowing. I am filled with gratitude that I'm slowly letting go, loving more and being loved more.

Carole

This chapter, "Bonding In the Eyes Comes with Caution," added a whole new dimension to eyes that I had not explored before. For me to look into someone's eyes in the past brought me a different feeling than Nancy experienced. When I look into someone's eyes, the fear comes from inside me as to what they are going to see. I never thought of the possibility that they would want to overtake me with their power. I had to think a long time why this was not so for me, because I do know I was taken advantage of many times. I had to replay many childhood scenes to be able to recognize that my offenders NEVER looked me square in the eye. I now realize that I could not even tell you, and be absolutely sure, the colors of my parents eyes.

I can not ever remember looking deeply into anyone's eyes in our household as I was growing up, just a quick glance seemed the way it was. Shame may have prevented this. I guess somehow if I did not see what was happening, I could block it out easier as a child. That would also seem true for my betrayers. Placement of the hands and tone of voice became much more important to me than eyes. The thought of this makes me sad that I was not able to look my offenders square in the eye and say, "No, you cannot take part of me with you!" The opportunity to do this has long passed. The hope of the future for our little ones makes me very excited. How wonderful in the many years to come if children could learn eyes are for soul bonding, transference of love, and seeing the beauty all around them.

EIGHT

Auming
Oneself
with Light

Cameron

*W*elcome today to all of our precious students. We wish to speak with you today about something that is quite necessary. As we open up to people and soul bond with them, they become quite attracted to us and us to them. What we have to do is be especially careful of holding our precious soul light inside of us, not letting it go, but letting it shine through to others. One way to do this that would be proper, is to visualize around your body a cylinder with many, many holes in it, or maybe a candle in a sphere with many holes. You light the candle and you can see light coming through, beautiful light radiating through. And that is really you, that is really your soul.

Now that you have found your soul and know it's there, we wish for your beauty to shine through to others, and we want you to give everyone love, that is for sure. But sometimes, we see people of great need wanting so much a part of you, wanting so much of your light. It's as if you have charisma. They draw to you. What we have to worry about, really, is them taking too much a part of you. They would not do this to hurt you in any way. They don't mean to do this, but it's almost like they're taking too much of your light, too much of your energy. So we would like to suggest that when you are in the presence of someone who is wounded or needy, so to speak, be aware if they are causing almost mental exhaustion for you. They may say, "Give me advice on this; give me advice on that. Please share with me your thoughts on this. Give me your ideas on that." Although they love to hear your lovely words, I'm sure, notice if sometimes after such a conversation you feel very tired.

Today we would like to teach you how not to let that happen, but how to still let your lovely light shine through to others. As we said in your visualization, it would be good if you could see yourself in a cylinder, such as we spoke or perhaps a colander, something like that. When you're in the presence of someone you think would be really interested in what you have to say or in some knowledge they think you have that they don't, visualize a cylinder all the way around your body. Right outside the cylinder see a piece of glass like plexiglass, or anything that is transparent. Then visualize your light coming through. That is really all you need, that is in a way guarding you. It is a way of letting your lovely soul show through to others. But this way, they really cannot take from you.

No one really wants to take from anyone else. Actually they don't mean to do this at all, you do know that. Just be very cautious the next time this happens. Listen very intently, and as you give part of your wisdom to someone, and you find yourself getting a little tired, a little exhausted, quickly, quickly put down your glass shield. Arm yourself with light. But in order to arm yourself, you must put a cylinder around the light as well, because it can be zapped from you so easily. And we certainly do not want people giving their light away because everyone has to find their own light, their own path. That would not be fair for either party.

We especially would like to bless those ones who are seeking the truth from you, who are seeking your light. We know that their path will be lessened by you sharing many things with them, and that is so good. And we also would like them eventually, when they find their own path and their own light, to do the same for themselves, shielding themselves. We don't want anyone grabbing from them either. So this is a two-way street, not that we're saying you have anything more precious than another, that's not what we're saying at all. We're just saying once you have found your path, once you have found your light, and you know you have, you must protect it as if it's a shining jewel. Don't give it away. That would not be a kindness for either one of you.

We would like to go for today, but we would like you to, in your mind, visualize your most radiant soul shining through. It can be seen in your eyes, but it could also radiate from your body to others. They can FEEL it and so this can and does need to be protected. So if you can think of this exercise, we would be so pleased for each of you. This way you can find and keep the holiness that you all have. We shall leave for now. Goodbye.

Tom

I have experienced many wonderful people who wanted me to help them and take away their pain. Of course, a priest is supposed to do this. I trained all of my life to be a priest and an educator. I loved God and my Lord Jesus with all of my heart and soul. I loved people, all people, and I so much loved helping them. This I knew was God's work for me. I felt love radiating through me to them. I was grateful that God was using me to help heal those around me.

At times, however, I became weary. A few were not satisfied with what I gave them. That weighed heavily on my heart. I could see in their eyes that they really wanted my love. They would come back time and again. I listened, shared my love with them, and expressed all the wisdom I knew. It wasn't enough. I felt they wanted my peace and my love. I saw a desperate search reflected in their eyes. Very soon I realized that I needed to protect myself. They wanted me to take away all of their pain. They did not understand why I could not. So many, I believed, expected miracles from me. They didn't know that each of us create our own miracles when we are ready for change to occur.

For those people, I was a disappointment. I understand now that it was really their own disappointment in themselves. I found it extremely difficult to reach a balance with this. I wanted to help and share my love, but I understood that I couldn't help them until they were ready to help themselves. It was a drain for me. Shortly before I came here, I began to see how unhappy these people were with themselves. I tried to give to them as I could and then to just love and bless them. My struggle with this lessened as I began to love myself more and realize that I didn't need to fix all of their problems. This saved some of my energy. My precious Nancy gave me that opening. Through loving her, I began to love myself more. She never knew this until I have spoken this to her now.

Each moment I began to give as much love and guidance as I could to people, then I had to let it go. It is really quite a harmful thing to do to a priest, you know, to expect miracles from them. God helps us as we help ourselves. As we truly open ourselves and become willing for change and true love to come into our lives, they will.

Nancy

When I reflect on Cameron's words about holding on to our precious light, I remember the times when I have felt my light energy being completely drained by other people. It's as if their needs were always more important than mine. Tremendous love and compassion filled me as well as a desire to ease their burdens. However, always after a certain point something inside of me felt an imbalance. It felt as if I was giving and not getting and I became weary. The light was being drained from my soul. My angels explained to me that I allowed myself to get into these situations. Now I believe that I never felt my needs were important and I spent my life giving, expecting nothing back. My soul longed for more love in my life. It has taken me years of therapy, hypnosis, and the radiant love of Jesus to teach me that I can love and serve other people, but also deserve love back. It's a sense of feeling worthy enough of the love. Because I did not get my needs met as a child, I grew up believing my needs were not important. Gratitude fills me now as I understand that because I finally love myself and I expect loving people around me, I get love automatically from everyone. It's as if an unspoken message goes out to those around me, "I love me, so please love and adore me also." This has become a reality for me. Oh, how glorious!

Carole

I know this chapter has so much good information for me. Often after I have done a reading for someone via Cameron, our conversations, after he leaves, turn into a great spiritual interchange. I love these special times with my friends.I have noted that Cameron hovers around for most of the conversation and drops a few tidbits into my head to enhance our exchange. These times are very easy for me, the words always just seem to be on the tip of my tongue. I thank

Cameron so much for helping to enlighten my thoughts. Lately I have noticed that I wish to carry on such conversations when he is not hovering quite so close. It seems I desire to have more and more spiritual conversations with people. It's amazing how people keep coming into my life.

I do find, though, after such conversations, I seem a little weary. According to Cameron, that seems to mean I have some light showing through, how exciting for me to think that I have possibly something to give to these people and they to me! I shall practice AGAIN arming myself with the cylinder to protect this precious light. Cameron taught Nancy and me about the cylinder and glass shell many, many months ago. He also used the words "angel film" for a visual type of protection. I used it often with good results, but somehow I must have been taking it for granted or just forgot. The reminder is just what I needed!

NINE

Peace Within You Becomes Apparent

Cameron

*H*ello again to our lovely students. We are now going to go on a journey that is so wonderful, and so peaceful. We now know that you have been able to soul bond with many people. Lovely, isn't it? We now are going to be on a journey to find our peace. When we find our peace we will be able to, as if in a ripple effect, generate this to many others. This is what it's all about, you know. We would love to see peace on earth in the next two hundred years or so. It would be so joyous for us to complete this mission.

We see you are able most of the time to look in someone's eyes and see their soul. But if for some reason you can't, try to look beyond the hurt, look beyond the hiding, for you will, in time, see their soul. Perhaps it may take two or three times, but you will see it, it is there. Often we see those who hide behind a defensive shield. They say, "No, you may not see my soul. I'm not worthy. I am not as precious as you think." But our mission today is to let everyone know there is a soul inside all people, including every single wounded person.

There is a beautiful shining soul in all, as if it is the most precious diamond in a jewelry store, it will be shining. We see ones on earth who find diamonds and jewels very precious, that is so. But there's nothing as precious as your soul. And once you've come to an understanding of that, and feel what you have inside of you is so precious, so revered, your life will be so beautiful. Do you remember we talked about the fan? If you were to remain with your fan open, with the window of your soul open, life would be miraculous. We wish for you all to find your reverence, all to find your beauty.

We are proud of all of you on earth. Oftentimes we see when you distance yourself from God, you are really not happy. We also see ones say, "Well, I don't believe in God, I don't believe in anything, any sort of source different than myself. I am the best. I am the one." We see people say that to themselves, but their soul doesn't really believe that, you know, that is their head getting involved in this. So we would like you today to try to understand and bless people who speak of that, people who speak of no God, no light, no one higher. They think when you die you just fall in a black hole of some sort; this is sad for us to think of.

We also see churches that want to put fear in ones. "If you are not good, you will go the hell," they say. "If you are good you will go to heaven." But what is good? What is it? Whose rules are those anyway? Are those earth rules? Who makes the rules? Who is good; who is bad? We see that everyone is good, everyone is precious. As we've said before, only their circumstances control where they are. That is really all it is.

And if we really CHOOSE our circumstances, so to speak, then we can also choose to be in one with God, in one with light, in one with the source that is all loving, whatever you choose to call it. If we wish to be in one with this, we must go with our fan open, open wide. At every turn, every corner be sure the fan is open. If it's closed at all, don't make that turn. Reflect, see what that corner has to tell you when the fan is closing. If you continue to always follow your fan, it would be absolutely certain that the window of your soul would be open in a very, very short time.

You cannot follow the guidance inside your chest-soul without the window to your soul eventually flapping open. If you could visualize shutters behind your eyeballs so to speak, they can close and open, you know. And we would like you to go with an open fan, with an open shutter; that would make us so proud, so happy, to see all your beautiful light, and all the beautiful wisdom that you have. For we all have our answers inside of us. We absolutely don't need anyone else for any of our answers. It's all stored right inside of us. But to get those answers we want the fan and shutters open; when you do that, you will be following the light, and your path. That really is how to find your path.

We oftentimes hear ones say, "I don't know how to find my path. I don't know where I'm going in life. What am I here for?" If you could keep the fan wide open, and your shutters wide open, which we say will flap open on its own when the fan is open for awhile, there will be no question, your path will come to you. You cannot help but find your path that way. You will be directed right to it. That is for sure.

So the lesson for today to our most, most precious students is, if you could, practice. I know you practice on your fan and we are so proud for you. But now we want everyone's beautiful soul to shine through. We do believe, though, that all of our special readers do have their fans open and do have their shutters open. What you could do is kind of a word of mouth to help others find their way. You know you could do that if you wish.

Just tell them to follow their heart, follow their heart-soul area. Decisions are in them, you know. All the answers are in them. If they were to follow with the fan open for awhile, the window to their soul will also flap open and then they will become whole. They will find their path. They won't need to grab and take from other people, you see. They will have their own answers. But it is, in a way, trusting oneself to know our answers are actually in there. They are. You are born with all your answers. You don't really need any outside help at all, only your connection with light, your connection with God, or your connection with any source higher than the wisdom of yourself. You would have to have your fan and shutters open; if you do that you will never have any questions at all, they will always be inside of you and that IS your path.

We wish to especially bless those ones today who are searching. It is scary. You think, "I can't answer these myself. I have to ask this person or that person because I know they have wisdom." But when you do that, it pulls from them a bit. But also, besides pulling from them what it does, it keeps you off your path. It is very good to have an exchange with a friend. We see that it is lovely and good, but we want to have a two-way exchange. That is what would get this world in a frame of mind of peace, of glory. And we wish to start that right here, if possible. It seems very simple, doesn't it? But, life is simple. We make life so complicated.

We will bless our special lovely ones for today, and we shall go.

Carole

As I write this today, I find myself in a situation that is very foreign to me. I know all this could have been avoided if I had only listened to my inner guidance. I find myself taking a person to small claims court to recapture monies due me.

The money does not seem nearly as important to me as trying to stop him from doing the same thing to other unsuspecting people. Upon further investigation, I learned he does this as a practice. I am just one in a long line of people seeking what's due them. How very sad for him!

We often vacation with our children and their families. These are such special times for us. I normally make arrangements for these trips. Usually I work with a rental agency in order to find a home big enough for all of us. We have never been disappointed in our accommodations. For spring break, a different type of scenery seemed to have everyone's approval. I scanned the newspapers and made a lot of calls. I found one home offered by a private party in the newspaper that seemed to fit our needs. I talked to a very pleasant gentleman. The house sounded perfect, everything we wished for in a rental home seemed to be there and more. Something felt strange. But I shrugged those feelings off. Weeks before our arrival, I sent him our final payment. A very foolish thing to do on my part. I should not have agreed to send all the money before arrival.

Within a few days I began to have more strange feelings about the house I had just rented, and him. I called him to obtain a little more information and found his phone was disconnected! Funny, I had just spoken to him five days before at that number. I only had a post office box address for him. What now? Was my vacation house or money gone forever? I was feeling very unsettled inside, just what was going on? I felt so silly for not checking this house out further. Why was I so trusting? I wanted to believe in him. In one of our conversations this man told me he was trustworthy. Why would he feel he had to tell me that, because he was not? What to do now? It really seemed too late to find another home on such short notice for such a popular vacation time as spring break.

In a few days the man called me and explained why his phone was no longer in service and gave directions to his rental home. Silly me, all was well, why did I even question that gnawing feeling inside of me? Everything was okay. Everything was settled in my head now.

Spring break was here. Everything was packed. Four cars were loaded to the brim with kids, skis, golf clubs, tennis rackets and more. We were on our way! This rental home was very secluded, and off the highway, down a winding gravel road and deep into the woods. As I spotted the large house in the clearing, a jolt went through me. I began to feel nervous for some reason. As I stepped foot in the house my heart started pounding. As everyone started unpacking, I was beginning to feel sick to my stomach. My daughter said that the same thing was happening to her. We all stopped what we were doing and started looking around. We were not sure what made the energy so bad in that house. It was filthy and hadn't been cleaned with care in many months. We noticed the cockroaches, unusual in this state. Spiders called it home; they were quite comfortable there.

The children said they wanted to leave. My grandson said he felt unsafe. Spending the night there, much less sleeping in the beds, seemed unthinkable. To us this house was definitely uninhabitable and very misrepresented. About this time the owner called to see if all was well. We told him our plight. He seemed most surprised, embarrassed, apologetic, and understanding and would send us our refund within the week. We have yet to see a penny. That was months ago.

The rush for all of us to get out of there astonished me. The cars were packed in record time. I felt an energy of such strength it almost pushed me out the door. AMAZING! Where to go now? We were blessed to find a home available for the week at our favorite resort. It housed twelve people. The opening, I'm sure, was not by chance.

I carried the black energy pit in my stomach, as did my daughter, for several hours. Upon arriving at our destination, I hit a pole and shattered the back window of my van. Another new experience for me. My first damage to a car. My lessons were taught hard that week, but I hope I learned them well. Listen, listen to my inner voice and feelings. Going only with my fan open during the search for our vacation home would have brought me peace instead of such an unsettling experience, if only I had listened.

My biggest sadness comes from allowing myself to become another of this man's victims. I do not like to be party to helping him bind his soul tighter. Facing off before the judge is not at all where I needed to feel whole. My hope is that I can face this gentleman who tried to do me a disservice and look deep into his eyes and possibly try to soul bond with him so that someday, he too, can find and know his preciousness through knowing we are all connected and all ONE.

Two months later: There is now a conclusion to this story. I was not given the opportunity to meet this man in court and make eye contact with him as I had hoped for before. He defaulted on responding in the prescribed time to our claim against him. We were sent papers signed by the judge stating that we now have the right to claim our money through his bank account, attach his wages or we could even now put a lien on his property. These options came up empty. As I scurried around with the judgment in hand to try for a different form of collection, I felt a tightness in my chest. It became apparent to me something was not feeling right. I stood somewhat reluctantly in the long DMV line to get a printout on his many cars.

It was curious but I realized that I did not want to have his cars impounded and sold after all. The thought of doing this gave me a sad feeling. I knew monies owed me would certainly come back to me when the cars were auctioned off.

My head said, "You've come this far, don't stop now! You can get what he owes you this way."

It was finally my turn at the counter. I requested owner information printouts from the DMV clerk. As she was handing me the papers I felt a profound shift stirring inside of me. I just knew I did not want to pursue this case any longer. A new-found strength as well as a peacefulness surrounded me.

How could this be, what was happening? My head kept trying to make sense and reason with that big feeling inside of me that said, "Drop this case!" The feeling was so strong that this time I listened and gave validity to it. What was this feeling all about? Were my lessons really over? "But you don't have your money yet," yelled my head. After some reflecting about all that had happened I knew my lessons were at a conclusion and they had been priceless!

I learned so much of value surrounding this whole situation. Four points became evident:

1. *Follow only with my fan open. If I had done that in the beginning when searching for our vacation home, none of this would have happened.*

2. *I had to develop and stay with my strong side to pursue the case through the courts. Being in that space was foreign and somewhat scary. I now know I have a strong side to tap into if needed.*

3. *I realize it is not my duty to save others from this man's ways, nor was it my job to help him find his path. I know we all must do this for ourselves.*

4. *I learned to give credence when I sensed that it was time to quit chasing all the avenues for payback. I know I can trust this sense in any situation now.*

When I felt my fan closing, I needed to stop what I was doing and take note, and in this situation I knew it meant to move on. The money owed is no longer an issue for me. I now realize it was only the vehicle to my priceless lessons. Since I have dropped this claim my fan is wide open and I feel wonderful!

My hope is that this man shall find his path of peace. Cameron suggested long ago that I add this happening to the book. I remember balking at the idea. I thought it was such "petty earth stuff," and besides I was not particularly proud that I had gotten myself wrapped up in it. I certainly didn't want to share this story in our book. However, Cameron's gentle suggestion came up again after he dictated this chapter. After pondering, I decided to write the story. Little did I know it was packed with so many profound lessons for me. Thank you, Cameron!

Nancy

Restlessness has been with me all of my life. I had to constantly keep busy. Just to be was not something I could do. This began to change slowly as I progressed through therapy, hypnosis, and group sessions. Now I understand that I was healing and reaching a peace within myself. For me it was a process of uncovering and searching deep within my soul to find what was making me nervous. My nervous energy was me running from me.

I've learned that our mode of operation of constant doing, whatever the form, indicates we are not in touch with our soul, are not able to just be, and are not at peace. My constant busyness prevented me from asking, "Am I at peace? Am I truly happy?" I had a gnawing feeling, especially in the last ten years, that I wasn't happy. Finally I listened and went for help.

Peace comes when we stop fighting what our soul wants us to do and we turn our lives over to God and get help with our childhood issues. Many times I've heard from people I know, "I don't have any childhood issues. This is just the way I am." If an individual is continually busy and relationships, work or health, are not in balance then there are often past childhood issues to look at. Why was I brave enough to deal with mine? God's grace is my only answer.

As I slowly got in touch with my feelings, found and allowed my soul to guide me, I noticed the earth more. Everything seemed to intensify. Getting in touch with my feelings intensified all of my senses. Music was more beautiful because I could feel it. Flowers were more beautiful because I could feel their beauty. People were also more beautiful because I felt their souls. Finally, I was at peace.

Pretty soon my desire to be busy seemed to go away and I could actually sit and read a book for long periods of time. Hours were filled with meditation as I allowed myself to float. It took a while to learn how to do this. My pattern for so long had been that if I tried to be still and close my eyes during the day, I'd think of everything I had to do. My soul began to let go and just be and trust that if I let go of control I would be okay. For me, it is crystal clear why I couldn't let go and just be. I didn't trust that I'd be okay. If I wasn't always in control, there was a good possibility something would happen to me, so I kept my guard up.

God sent angels to help me trust and guide me to peace. Now I understand that I had to get help with my childhood issues and release the hurt within me before I could find the trust and deep peace that I feel now. I couldn't find God and Jesus because I was too busy running away from me. Running meant I didn't have to feel or remember. To remember was to find the truth. It wasn't as bad as I thought it would be, in fact, it set me free. By allowing myself to go through the process, I let go and finally found God. I do have times, periodically, when fear sets in, but those moments don't last. God and Jesus help me then. Afterwards I am able to return the love and peace I feel. My most profound experience of Jesus helping me occurred recently.

Deep sorrow for the loss of Tom washed over me as he expressed his wisdom through this book. I remembered what a beautiful gift he was to earth, how much everyone loved him and what an inspiration he was to us all. The reality of being totally in touch with my feelings meant that my feelings intensified, including my sadness. Soon I began to realize that I hadn't grieved Tom's death. My ability to feel at the time of Tom's death was limited. Now I began that experience and became overcome with grief.

Deciding that I needed help with my grief, I took a trip to the University of Portland and the chapel that Tom so dearly loved. As I sat there, my heart was so heavy I felt I couldn't breathe. "Jesus, please give me strength," I prayed. Something amazing happened which I still cannot explain I felt a pull, a lifting. My heart didn't ache anymore. I was stunned.

This is the most profound help I had ever received. In the past I have felt tremendous love from God and Jesus but nothing like this. Jesus took that pain from me, and I felt at peace. My whole being changed and I was calm again. It was a floating sensation. My gratitude was overwhelming.

I am grateful that my life is filled with peace. When moments occur when I don't feel at peace, I know what to do to get it back. Life is a glorious journey!

Tom

My entire life was spent in contemplative prayer and the study of religious thought. Several times in my life I had experienced moments of profound love from my Lord Jesus. These times gave me great peace. I knew I was loved and could feel God's love. It helped me understand that my mission was to help others. This belief replaced the hurt that occured in my childhood. I immersed myself in church duties to somehow seek God's forgiveness. Surely if I followed God's path all of my life and devoted myself to His work, I would be worthy and free of shame. I did not understand this during my life. I do now.

I was driven all of my life. As I achieved one goal, it was quickly replaced by another; undergraduate, graduate, pastoral work, community work, and on and on. I had a great amount of love within me that I wanted to share with others.

The truth is I was hiding. I became so busy that I wouldn't have to feel. I was running away from myself. On one level I felt secure in my relationship with God. It was my relationship with people that was not balanced. The priesthood allowed me to be what my mother and father wanted: perfect, God's chosen one. I loved my church and my religious training; however, for all priests, there is a human side too. Without expressing it we are unbalanced.

My childhood was quite difficult. There was little love in our home. Our existence was based on guilt and shame. Daily my mother asked forgiveness of God for our sinful ways and expected me to pray with her. I got the message early on that I was bad. From constantly hearing "Shame on you," and "We must ask for God's forgiveness," I soon came to the conclusion that I was bad. I was shameful. Now I understand that this beautiful woman was just trying to erase her own guilt for what she was doing to her children. I am grateful to her for helping me find God and my Lord Jesus at a very early age. But the guilt and shame became a shackle during my life. God reached me throughout my life and let me know I was loved.

Through my connection with God I was able to achieve a certain level of understanding and compassion. It was this that I believe people felt from me. At a deeper level, however, I did not feel worthy of unconditional love and I was not completely at peace. I kept myself busy.

Something happened to me that woke up my personal feelings. Nancy came into my life. I never spoke a word or gave her a hint at the growing feeling of love I felt. I knew it was not possible for me to express my inner feelings to her due to being a priest. But the joy she radiated was a magnet to me. I enjoyed working beside her. Even an unspoken love is a magnificent thing.

I began to realize that I had never experienced the joy of love as a child. My life had been so rigid and programmed before. Now I felt like opening up. That's what love did to me. This experience of loving allowed me to heal from my childhood pain. The love I received from God and my Lord was magnificent, but obviously God wanted me to feel love for a person or Nancy would not have been brought into my life. It became clear that there was a piece missing in my life. A piece I could not have.

Now I am at peace. Not just because I am here. The love I experience here is beyond my hopes. I am filled with light and love. My Lord Jesus is always with me. However, He has given me the opportunity to be with Nancy from another dimension so that I can heal further. Do you understand that after we die the healing continues? As we feel worthy we ascend to a closer relationship with God. Soon

I am going to ascend to a different level. My soul is eager for this growth.

I carried the pain I felt on earth from my childhood and from being unable to be with Nancy. Now our relationship is part of the healing and moves both of us closer to God. She has helped me remember and deal with feelings from my childhood. I feel free at last. Now I am able to express my love for her and not feel shameful. You know it's shameful on earth for a priest to love a woman. How sad that is, as it destroys the soul and blocks God's intention of learning to love and feel through relationships.

God has explained that my mission in this book is to carry His message to earth through the example of my life and pain. It is my desire to bring change to the Catholic church. God is asking for all of his children to be allowed to experience all of life's lessons and opportunities. He wants us to be allowed to feel and love each other.

I have found that human relationships combined with religious study, practices and meditation can bring an individual to wholeness and peace. One without the other doesn't work. The combining of our spiritual and the human side is what the earth experience is all about. These practices elevate our souls and are part of the divine plan. Somehow in our history this became confused. God is asking for a change to what He originally intended.

Miracles Become Your Companion

Cameron

*W*e wish today to continue our wonderful journey with our students. We find that when you can go through your life with shutters open in back of eyes and fan open in the chest area, miracles come to you. Often people think miracles are just for certain people, certain lucky people. They say, "Oh, a hand of God must be in that." Or, if they like to put something scientific into it, they would say, "Oh, it has another meaning; it couldn't possibly be God, it just happened." They try to explain it away in terms their head can understand. But we wish to offer to you today the fact that miracles can happen to you daily. And they will happen to you daily if you are open to them.

Miracle is a wonderful word, isn't it? Really, all it means is something joyous has happened. People would say something like, "Oh, I haven't been sick in so long," and they might say, "It's a miracle." But it's not that, you have just not pulled illness into you. You have remained on your path, with your shutters and fan open. You can't help but be healthy with them open. We find illness is quite big on earth. It distracts people often in their head. It consumes their thoughts and bodies sometimes.

Illness is very important to some people. It gets them what they want. It can also be a form of control for others. That seems strange, doesn't it? But you can, in fact, control others by your own illness, because then others have to give their time for you. They have to take away from their own path and serve you when you are ill. They usually do this out of guilt. It is sad to see that. We see this pattern often on earth.

People would serve a kindness to others by not allowing themselves to so frequently explain their ills. This doesn't do anything for the other person. They might want to comfort you, that would be proper, that would be okay. But to constantly, constantly say to some people, "I have this hurt, I have that hurt. Oh, I picked up the flu. I did this and that." What is that? Why would you burden someone with that? That is hard for us to understand. But some people get so into the mode of having illness as a way of getting attention, that it becomes a habit. They don't know how to get out of it. Their soul does not want to be ill.

Your body does not need to hurt and ache, we know that. We want to say when you find your path, and we think you can, illness will NOT become a part of you. As if a miracle had happened you say, "Here I am, eighty years old, yet no illness. Why, why me? What is it about me that I am not ill?" The simplest answer for that is to say you are on your path. Your path does not allow any illness to be part of you.

We often see the way people die is from a major illness. It's really that their soul is dying. It's not that their body wants to get sick and then eventually have their heart or lungs stop. What is this thing called illness? Do you know that we were made by God, and in the wonderful wisdom of our Creator, the plan was for us to die, just as if we went to sleep. When you are very old at a time when all of your lessons are done, deep into your life, that is the proper way. God does not want anyone to suffer.

People used to live years, years, years longer in biblical times. We do want to note at this time, that today we often see people born with many illnesses. Have you ever wondered about that? How can a baby have such a terrible disease? How can a baby be born with something? What did they ever, ever do to deserve this? That is probably what you would ask. Really, with this theory we are giving to you, it doesn't make sense does it? But we wish to tell you at this time that babies come with illness into life when they are trying to deal with things from another past life. And they have made a conscious choice to do that, a conscious choice to live out an illness. They are learning much in their soul, even as a very tiny infant.

We also see young people draw into themselves an illness and leave earth before their time. The reason for this could be something they were drawing from a past life, or it could be something that they decided to draw into themselves to help teach someone of close proximity to them, perhaps a lesson about illness. It could also be that earth is so harsh for them that they think they want an escape route. They draw that illness energy into themselves.

If we had our shutters open in back of the eyes and fan open in the chest-soul area, there would be no need for illness, no need at all. What would the doctors do? What would the hospitals do if this were really so? This is a big concern, isn't it? We see the earth has been very affected by the medical field. Would it be possible in say two hundred years or so that this was obsolete? That there was actually no need for medical services! How could that be? Illness is such a big part of the earth. It stretches the mind, doesn't it, to think this could possibly happen. God does not want anyone to be ill. Why have we drawn that into us? Curious, isn't it?

We hope a very tiny seed can be planted today for people to just think about it, even a little bit, that's all we're asking. We are not asking for a great reform today, not at all, just think about your illness a little. Perhaps then when something comes into your mind such as, "maybe I will get that illness." Try to replace it, if possible, with a very happy thought, just see what will happen. See how your body will respond to that. Just try.

We do not see that there will be a big change on earth in the illness area in a couple of centuries. But when it does happen, people will have to read about it in history books. They won't even know what you are talking about. This will happen. It seems strange, doesn't it, because illness is such a big part of the world today. Perhaps some of you listening or reading this today will have the opportunity to come back to earth in a few hundred years and see how it is. It will be a different world, we can guarantee that! Excuse us a minute if we get excited about looking into the future because to have no illness on earth would be for us a miracle.

And so what we would like to do is integrate into our wonderful students that miracles can happen. They can happen in your body by you being free of illness. They can happen by releasing you from a pain, a mental pain. Many things could happen. Often when we see people with a heavy illness, like not being able to walk and then something happens and they are able to walk, then people say, "It's a miracle." That is not really what is happening at all.

What's happening is their soul says, "I will not accept this illness anymore. I will get rid of it." So we use our lovely word "miracle" since it can mean so much, can't it? You see a miracle, you think, is something that can ONLY occur from an outside source, something outside of you has to have caused it. You say, "God must have done that, Jesus must have done it, what is it that did this?"

So what we would like for you lovely ones to understand today is that the miracles are IN YOU. They are not coming from outside. Of course, they are coming with God's precious hand on them, but God is in all of you, every one of you. We all are connected. You may think if miracles come from outside your body, then Jesus must have done it. How could that be so? Jesus is the same as you, you're as capable. Do you see what we are trying to say today? Miracles begin in you, become one with you. They can happen daily to you.

If you ask for something and you really want to have it as part of you, it will happen, if this is for the goodness of your soul. You do not have to wait for miracles to happen, so to speak, from outside of your body. It does not have to be for a chosen few, it can be for you. It can be for anybody. It can be for your next-door neighbor, it can be for ANYBODY. We just have to believe. When we are on our path with the shutters and fan open, they happen constantly.

We'd like to leave you with a thought today that YOU ARE A MIRACLE. God sees you all as a miracle. Jesus sees you all as a miracle and we see you all as a miracle. You are all lovely and we are very blessed today to be speaking to you dear ones. Goodbye.

Carole

My self-assigned job for this book is to take the cassette tape on which Cameron has dictated the chapter, put it in a player with headphones and transfer the spoken words to longhand on paper. Although this is sometimes tedious and time consuming, I love this job. This way I can really get in touch with Cameron's words. Channeling the chapters in this book is so different for me than doing a reading for someone. While Cameron is dictating the book, I hear no conversations among the angels, nor do I see any pictures or feel any feelings. I am not interacting in my mind with the words he is speaking. I also remember little of what he says and with no pictures for my memory to draw upon, everything seems blank. This style is very different for me. I feel like I am on a journey each time I put the headphones to my ears.

As I was listening and writing the words of this chapter, chills came over me. I'm amazed at how healing this book is for me. Exposing the hidden parts of my mind is so freeing. As far back as I can remember, illness and operations were a big part of my world. They made me feel important and cared for. This started at the early age of six and lasted until I was in my late forties. It's a little embarrassing and hard to admit that I looked forward to being in the hospital. The very first thought that crossed my mind upon entering was that I would be taken care of and my mother would visit and bring me flowers. Many of my needs from her were not met in daily life. So somewhere in my being, her hospital visits seemed to make up for some of it and brought me comfort. Creating kidney stones was my vehicle to be admitted in for care. Hospitals take this condition seriously and act swiftly to make you comfortable. Ah, I loved the attention. I felt so comforted. The degree of pain made no difference to me. People were responding to my needs. As the years passed, the kidney stones were just part of the long list of conditions within my body. I could claim quite a collection of operations and illnesses by my late forties. Some days my body just seemed to be filled with aches and pains. Maybe this happens when you are nearing fifty! My parents certainly have had their share of illnesses. Maybe it just runs in the family, I thought.

When I started my therapy I had quite a list of body ills. What amazes me to this day is that as my childhood memories bubbled up, my ills went with them. My last operation was a curious one, a very large boil on my toe. As I entered the hospital for this last trip under the knife, my body seemed to be boiling over, I could just feel it. Was it my trapped memories? They emerged with rapid succession in the next few weeks. This seems very profound to me.

It was interesting for me to learn that I did not have to feel old or be sick just because I was in middle age. I can now see I have no need for any illness. The thought of ever having an operation seems foreign to me. I do believe, though, if I ever call an illness into me again that I will have the need to question myself as to why I pulled this into my energy and for what purpose. I hope that day will never come.

Near the end of my therapy and for two years after, I had not one ache, pain, or illness of any sort. A miracle had happened! I had to readjust my thoughts, though, that illness no longer served a purpose for me. I was getting used to being pain-free and felt so wonderful and so alive.

Then it happened. Nearly one year ago today I had a stroke, hours later, I had another. As I lay in the emergency room of the hospital, I felt like I was in slow motion. My speech was slurred, motor skills poor with both sides of my body affected and short term memory dulled. I was 51 years old. What happened? It seemed to me that everyone was behind several sheets of glass. Everything seemed so untouchable.

Is this what it feels like when you are dying? The possibility of another stroke may be imminent, the doctors said. That did not happen. I was sent home.

Speech, occupational, and motor skills therapists would be sent to my home when I was strong enough. How could this be? I wanted no part of illness, why did I have these strokes? I thought I finally had my life on a path that did not seek the needs of doctors and hospitals. What happened?

As the months droned on at home I struggled to eat with a spoon and fork, use a pencil, curl my hair, brush my teeth, and color in the lines. I learned to walk and talk all over again. The more I learned, the more I realized what a miracle these strokes had been for me. I was learning all the skills a child learns at home, but this time I was in a loving, nurturing environment and not in a dysfunctional home. I needed to redo my childhood through the loving hands of these therapists. What a gift I had been given. Thank you, God!

But what I learned so deeply and what became a valuable lesson for me is to have patience with those who cannot speak at a pace I think necessary, and not to stare at someone who cannot walk without a wavering stride. I realized never to talk over those that have slurred speech and especially not to pretend they are not there. I have been in a body such as this and the stares cut deep. The upturned eyes of impatience were so deflating for me. The most precious gift that I learned from this was when I deemed myself useless, my husband, children, and grandchildren saw my wholeness and showed me their unconditional love. It still brings me great joy and awe to think how my renewal strokes helped me to find my path of wholeness.

The doctors are unsure what caused the strokes. One of the many possibilities is that years of stress can cause certain areas to constrict at the base of the brain stem. All I need to know is that one year later I have come full circle in my healing with a new awareness. Within six months I had my "wheels" back. My first venture on the freeway was mind boggling. WHERE was everyone going and WHY were they going so fast? It made little sense. I felt there must be more important things in life than just scurrying around. But soon I became part of the flow of traffic. I had to keep up! For six months I was able to go at my pace and not the pace that traffic or anything else demanded. Part of me longs for that again. I have now been reacquainted with my tennis racket and have just taken up golf lessons, and I'm back to full activity.

It may be interesting to note Cameron would not come through me for the many months I was recuperating. He did, though, let me know that he would watch over me and hover close around me and return to channeling when I was stronger. When I had sufficient strength Cameron came through as promised and said the strokes were a necessary part of my healing. I had drawn them into me. I feel truly blessed to have learned my lessons this way. For me, it was a miracle!

Tom

Miracles were a part of my life as a priest. Miracles in myself as well as other people. The more I witnessed miracles, the more my faith deepened. I felt such profound awe in it all. My first miracle was as a young boy. I was extremely upset one day because of an argument that my sister and mother had. I tried to tell my mother to stop, but she said, "Go to your room." I went to my room and cried, then I prayed. I knew that God could help; I knew He would. An overwhelming feeling of love entered my room and then, I saw Jesus. I knew it was Jesus. He said, "Go in peace. All is as it should be. I will help and protect your sister." In that moment all of my fear vanished; I felt peaceful. I don't know what surprised me more, the vision of Jesus or the feeling of love and peace.

I was never the same after that. To actually see my Lord and feel his loving presence profoundly touched me. Even as a child I understood that He would take care of my sister. It relieved me of the burden I felt. It seemed to erase my guilt for never being able to prevent her suffering. My faith increased. It was then that I knew I wanted to be a priest.

Throughout my life I've witnessed miracles happening around me. People would tell me stories of being healed from sickness or being saved from danger. People frequently came and asked me to heal them. These were desperate individuals. Those who had miracles happen to them never asked me for miracles. They knew and believed miracles could happen to them. Because of their belief, miracles did happen. I would often ponder the differences. The magic ingredient was faith, faith in a higher power beyond ourselves, faith and a belief that anything is possible.

Those with little faith seemed confined to a life of fear and doubt. "I can't. Nothing can change. I'll believe it when I see it." All of these words filled their hearts. These people were destined to an existence of hardship and struggle. I saw a pattern: doubt and fear equaled hardship and struggle.

Many people have a strong faith, but they haven't healed from childhood wounds, so their lives remain filled with hardship and struggle. The more we heal and rid our lives of fear, the more God is allowed to work in our lives and miracles do occur.

Did you know that wanting to be in control, staying busy or feeling frequent bouts of anger are really indications that we are fearful? We're fearful of facing ourselves and being honest about our feelings. Miracles can't happen when our lives are filled with fear.

Letting go, asking for help, and believing help is available is what brings miracles. I witnessed this in myself and others who had miracles happen to them. When we finally say, "God, I can't do this anymore; I need help!" That's when change happens and the pathway of miracles opens to us.

Nancy

I believe what happened to me in the chapel was a miracle. There was such a profound shift in the way that I felt that I was startled. My immediate reaction was to believe that the chapel was a very sacred and holy place. However, since that moment I have asked Jesus to help me many times, and I've experienced the shift again.

It is not the place; it is within me and can occur any time and anyplace. My logical mind cannot explain what happened; I have a tendency to want to figure out what happened. How could I feel so much sadness and be hurting so deeply and then in an instant, it is gone? What occurs? My logical mind has no explanation for what happened to me physically.

About the time I experienced these miracles in my life, I also visited a vortex. There are numerous locations on earth called vortexes. These are places where there is a difference in the electromagnetic fields. The normal physical laws as we know them do not apply. The properties of gravity act differently. Things appear to change size, what we see is the opposite of what we think it should be. A ball rolled back to me when I rolled it down a hill. The ball was not a trick ball, but most people who witness that do not believe it.

This was a perfect experience for me at this time for the book. It was very difficult for the people around me at the vortex to believe it could be real. They could not understand it; therefore, it must not be real. These moments expand our minds and offer us opportunities to grow. Just because we can't explain or understand doesn't mean something is not real or the truth.

Miracles are happening to me because I believe they can, even though I do not understand how. I'm not sure where my deep, deep faith has come from, but I totally believe anything is possible in my life. When I pray for help I know that something or someone can and will help me. For me, I believe it to be God, Jesus, and my angels. Incidents happen constantly to me where I ask for help and it comes almost immediately. Help comes in relieving me of my pain and in physical things as well. I ask for the resources I need, both in my personal life and in my professional life, and they appear. Therein lies the concept of faith. If we believe it to be, it will be.

Instead of "Show me and then I will believe," I understand that when I believe, truly believe, that's when I am shown, not before. My thinking had to change before the miracles could begin to happen and love and abundance could enter my life.

Circle With Two Sides Becomes Proper

Cameron

*W*elcome today to our precious students. We wish to tell you about something that seems a bit confusing. Can you think about a circle that would have two sides to it? A circle is a continuous thing, is it not? How could it have two opposite sides? What does that mean?

What we are talking about here is our wonderful people. Our wonderful people on earth today are who we are talking about. We are talking about our male-female people. You are both, you know. Does that make sense to you? You have to be both to become one. You have to have an agreeance in your body, an agreeance of male-female energy to become a whole. Does that make sense to you?

It seems on earth that people want to be proper for male or female. They can't think how you could be both and be one whole. That doesn't make sense, does it? The proper way is to have a balance of each to compliment each other. The

107

male energy wishes for a soft side AND wishes for a tougher side. When you say tougher, you think of male energy. Why is that? What does that really mean? The female we think is always soft. Sometimes people even think the female is to be taken care of by the male. How could one be whole that way, if taken care of by others?

What we wish to teach you today is that the balance is what is so supreme. That is what we are all gasping for as if to get air. Sometimes we get smothered by ones who are a stronger energy than us. How do we hold our own, how do we do that? To be a complete whole you have to have a balance of each, half and half, male and female. Often people are in fear and the only way they can get out of fear, they think, is to be controlling. When they do this, they adopt a male energy. They think this gives them a lot of strength and a lot of power, but underneath it all, there is fear. That brings us a lot of heartache today.

Often the feminine side is described as someone who can sit back and let the stronger energy take care of things. What does it do for you if you are out of balance, if one is stronger than the other? What could you possibly get out of life? We must make our own decisions. We must not let anyone push us or shame us into their decisions that THEY think are better for us. We would like this to be our lesson today.

If we went with our fan open we would never have to be strong or weak, or adopt a male OR a female energy. Strong or weak, male-female energy is really just an illusion of your mind. We don't see males as any stronger, females as any weaker. We see them as absolutely the same. Male energy may have certain properties that the female energy docs not. But they compliment each other, always compliment each other. We never want one to out-balance the other.

We see many women on earth become very weak. They

say, "Oh, I can't do that, it is a male thing." Who made up those rules? Are those earthlings who do that? Who says this is a male thing, this is a female thing? Who says that? When you buy into that, it makes that part of your energy very weak. We do not see any determination that should cause a male or female to be any different at all. The only difference we see is that the male is structured differently, the muscles are different. So one might think, if the muscles are different, then the work could be different. That might be so. But to have someone map their life because they are male or female and only stay in that energy, does not bring them to a full circle. It must be a balance.

Today we could explore how to get a balance. One way of doing this, we see, could be to start in the work place. It has become apparent to us that some think, well, a man must run the country, you see, he is stronger. How could that be? He started out the same, all the same beautiful seed of light. The male-female seed of light is the same, neither are stronger. Stronger body only, but that is all. Would it be possible, in maybe a hundred years or so, that we might see a female running the United States and some other countries, maybe before, maybe way before? That would be a delight to us. This would bring a big reverence to women. We see on earth that reverence is not big for women, in some countries for sure.

Could we get a balance? How could we all love each other and all be one if we are not all in balance? Somehow because the male is a stronger body, the earth has adopted him as a stronger person, maybe even a better person. Why is that? Do you think we could possibly change that? We see, excuse us for saying, that some of the problem is that women often ALLOW that to happen. They allow men to take the forefront because they say, "I am the weaker, I will let them make the decisions." But what does that do to your soul? Today we would only like to plant a seed, and that seed would be for women to think, "I am absolutely the same," for men to think, "I am absolutely the same."

In marriage we often see there is an unconscious agreement based on human heritage, that the male should prevail, because he is thought to be the stronger. Do you think possibly that women could revere themselves? And men revere themselves enough to realize that it needs to be a decision made by two, no one is stronger. That could go into the work place. It could go so many places. We see there needs to be quite a reform in the work place. Men usually get higher positions. We even see they are getting paid more for the same positions. How can that be equal? If that is so then something is almost saying women are less than. How could that be? Oftentimes we see women of great power are disliked. Why is that? We don't like their strength? This needs to be examined further, don't you think? Only today a very tiny seed is to be planted, a seed of thought really. We don't expect any reform, just some thought.

If our mission truly is to get everyone in a circle of wholeness, then there must be change. We see the pillars of earth are really the males. We need for everyone to be a pillar, their own pillar. Could there be just a thought change, and maybe when a big reform comes in a couple of centuries or so, change will happen, the seed will be planted.

Perhaps we could teach our children that women are as precious as men, men as precious as women, no less, no more. Why is it that women should have softer qualities? Do you think they can be more emotional? It is not proper, some people think, for men to be so emotional. Why should they be robbed of that part of themselves? Why should they be shunned for that?

We often see fathers saying to young men growing up, "Be strong, be tough." How could we change that? We must allow these men to FEEL all their feelings. We do have a very reverend priest on our side. He was told to be tough, and that he needed to put his feelings aside for priesthood. This caused him great dismay. We do believe his part in this book is big. He will talk of this. You will learn much from him. He is blessed heavily for the mission in this book. He has a highly recognized name in his church. This is very necessary for reform to have him widely known. He is adorned for his mission.

We would like to leave you with a thought today. Everyone is just as precious as everyone else, male or female, There is no difference whatsoever. We are all full circle. For everyone to find their potential, they must have a male-female side to them, totally equal. They must experience all their feelings. This is where our wonderful priest comes in. He shall share much with you. We'll bless you for today. Goodbye.

Tom

I was made to feel shameful as a child for feeling any emotion. My strict upbringing encouraged continual prayer and self sacrifice. I soon learned that my needs and feelings were not important. To express my own needs or feelings was considered a weakness. My father would say, "It's up to you to be strong and take care of your mother and sister while I am away." My religious training emphasized that we are weak and must ask God for forgiveness. Forgiveness for what? I wasn't bad, I hadn't hurt anyone. My parents would not tolerate tears from me. My early spiritual teachers told me God would help me and that I needed to be strong and not cry.

What an awful thing to do to a child. I stopped feeling. I encountered so many roadblocks at home and at church for showing my emotions that pretty soon I understood that I was bad. I showed too much emotion. I was reminded that priests were supposed to be strong and sacrifice themselves while serving God. That was the ultimate ideal, the ability to totally transcend one's own feelings and desires and serve other people and God.

Where did this value come from? I had the normal range of emotions of a child. I felt both joy and a deep sadness. It was natural for me to express myself. Soon however, I was made to understand that this was not God's way.

As a priest I understood that I was expected to discipline myself to hide my emotions. How could we do this to priests? Feeling totally human and experiencing all of life is what is expected of us while we are on earth. That is the gift. To deny feeling means to deny our feminine side. The only way I could survive was to somehow attempt at releasing emotions through hard work and service. I was driven, I became strong and achieved one goal after another. However, I did not feel whole. On rare occassions a few close friends loved me enough to allow me to be me. With them I was able to express my true emotions. These brief moments helped me survive in my rigid enviroment.

My father taught me as a child that I must be a man and not cry. My church taught me that I must sacrifice myself for God. Slowly, as I progressed along my path, and was maturing and feeling deeper, I felt my soul straining to be free of the strict confinements of the priesthood.

I received guidance from my Lord that went against Catholic doctrine on a number of issues. What if my passion was to help bring change and more love into our strict life? I knew that my Lord wanted this, however there were few avenues open for me to express these ideas. They did not fit into the doctrine at that time. I began to feel stifled. There seemed to be little passion in those around me. How could I express my ideas that would bring change to my beloved church? I loved the Catholic Church and wanted to help make it better. I perceived an emptiness in some of the leaders of my church. They seemed to be searching as well. Because I was struggling and afraid, I allowed others to dictate my beliefs and lifestyle.

When I was asked to be on the Board of Trustees of Notre Dame, I saw a flicker of interest in me and my leadership abilities. Perhaps I could effect some change by being at a larger university? I felt change was necessary within the Catholic faith. However, this was not to be how I could best effect change. I realize now my path is through this book, not through Notre Dame University. God presented opportunities for me to speak my truth to our religious leaders. However, I never felt comfortable enough to totally express my feelings. Fear and shame crept in. Now I know God wanted me to be genuine. My soul wanted to express the real me including my feelings. To hide and continue on as if I totally believed in everything my church believed caused great internal turmoil. However, I ignored my deepest beliefs and simply chose not to be me or express myself. I was afraid. I was a coward.

We can't hide forever. My Lord wanted me to be true to myself and express myself honestly. The longer we hide and the more opportunities we pass up to be real, the more it takes to get our attention. For some, the wake-up call is a stroke, a heart attack, a divorce, a business failure, etc.

For me it was Nancy. This was absolutely the worst thing that could happen to a priest. It took something profound to move me. God brought me a person so beautiful and filled with so much love that I could no longer remain numb. She broke through all of that by simply filling the world around her with joy. I hope many of you have the opportunity to know Nancy. You will understand why I love her so. There is a radiance about her; she is filled much more than I with the agape love that people said I had. I sensed then some

thing extraordinary about her. She loved everyone and expressed that. That, among other things, is why I loved her,
especially her openness in expressing emotions. She seemed
so real. It was refreshing.

I would wait as long as it took and travel through dimensions to be with her. I am now. I express all of my feelings
now. I have totally changed. I am no longer afraid. She loves
me back. She is my angel. Finally, I am in balance. For so
many years I was doing and achieving but not expressing
my true feelings. I am proud of what I accomplished on earth.
However, I was not allowed in my position to express all of
me and be whole. My circle is complete. The interesting fact
is that I had to leave earth in order to do this.

My request now is that this not be necessary for other priests.
We have too many wonderful souls who love God and Jesus
and who are also longing to be whole on earth. I ask the pa-
pal council to have enough courage to trust that things will
not completely fall apart if they examine these aspects of
Catholic doctrine. Is the church allowing priests and all pa-
rishioners to be the best they can be? Is it allowing individuals to follow their own path or does it try to control and dictate? People must fall down, learn, and then find God themselves.

Religious leaders are on earth to guide and inspire, not to
control and dictate. Excessive rules and dogmas destroy the
soul. It destroyed my soul. I had to be free to become whole.
Nancy is one of the most profoundly spiritual people I have
ever known. Her deep faith and courage inspire all around
her. She empowers more people with her love and faith than
most religious leaders I know. How can this be? She has little
or no religious training in her life. Her awakening occurred
only a few years ago. She found the light herself. Many were
her teachers, but always she chose her own way. She was
and will continue to lead more people to loving themselves

and to loving God than many of our own "chosen" ones.

Would my own church shun her because she did not follow their path? Would they refuse to believe her or this book because it dares to speak the truth and be honest? She is brave enough to speak the truth in this book knowing full well the controversy it will bring. She knows God has spoken to her to do this. She trusts that guidance.

I will be ascending very soon. We've only just found each other, and now we must separate again. Sharing so much love now we both wonder at times if we can do this. However, it is my choice to move closer to God and ascend. Do you understand that growth and deepening does not end with death on earth? It continues. I am continually growing. Just because I'm not embodied does not mean I do not feel and am not the same entity. Nancy was a gift to me to become whole. My love for her will continue through eternity as I move forward on my journey to oneness with God.

Nancy

I have had to be very strong all my life in order to be a survivor, not a victim. Now I realize that in order to survive I was using my male energy. That energy was my organizing, doing, striving, surviving, and controlling side. This energy allowed me to succeed in almost everything I did, but was not working for healthy balanced relationships with others. No one could get close or would want to because I was so strong and could be too overpowering.

Over the past three years I noticed myself changing as I explored within, remembered my past, experienced the feelings around that past and then slowly began to heal. A peaceful feeling came over me as I began to be comfortable with myself. I enjoyed being alone and just "being" rather than "doing."

Cameron said that my feminine was emerging. How exciting! There was an entirely other me in me, I had a softer side, very feeling, more reflective, that wanted to be taken care of and be quiet. The moments I enjoyed the most were when I allowed this energy to emerge. As I began to find this side of me I realized I was much happier. I didn't totally lose my masculine side, it simply calmed down a little and came into balance. Instead of giving and doing for everyone, I began to desire for myself. My soul wanted relationships that were a balance between giving and taking.

With Cameron's help, I became aware that in all of my close relationships with others, I had received very little back. I had given, expecting and getting little in return. My feminine aspect began to get frustrated and desired love in return. Cameron explained that my masculine energy has served me well in my life and has allowed me to survive. However, we all reach a point in our lives when we are out of balance, one way or another, and our lives are not in harmony and our relationships with people are not satisfying.

After my divorce, I dated, but I realized that I was not receiving the love I wanted. Cameron helped me understand that if I was not getting what I wanted out of life, it was ME that had to change, not other people around me. My masculine was still so strong that it was drawing people to me who gained strength from me rather than those who would give and express love.

I prayed for God to help my feminine emerge so that I could be balanced. It was hard for people to give to me because I was so strong. I was preventing the very thing I wanted, loving balanced relationships. Almost immediately opportunities to use my feminine energy arose. My bank account became totally out of balance due to a bank error. Instead of trying to fix it, I asked for help. It was hard to ask.

Another angelic energy appeared who was sent to assist me in opening my feminine side; he pampered me. Learning to accept this and receive was a new experience for me. Pretty soon new friends appeared who also gave to me. This led to an entirely new way of being. How could I allow someone to love and give to me if I wasn't comfortable with receiving and was afraid to open up? Suddenly I understood why I had never had loving relationships in my life.

I began to change. Love began to come from everyone and everywhere. Even my children responded differently and it felt wonderful. Then Tom came to me. His beautiful loving energy flowed around me. Instantly, I knew it was him. Even though I couldn't see him, I could feel his spirit and hear him. Remembering what he was like on earth, I realized that he was the same in spirit form.

Tom was the most beautiful person I had ever known on earth. His capacity to love others stunned all of us who worked with him. Without ever a word spoken, his love poured into everyone around him and empowered all of us. His delightful sense of humor, quiet strength and patience endeared us to him. After his death I felt honored to have known and worked with him. No one had ever inspired me more in my life. Even though I never had any conversations with him on earth about his beliefs, I felt his deep spirituality. We all felt God's presence in him.

I couldn't believe it when he came to me. I felt his deep feelings for me and I was shocked. There were so many layers I had to work through in my beliefs to even be able to believe and accept this. I already believed in the concept of angels. More evolution of my knowing needed to happen before I could understand that angels have feelings and are still growing even though they are not in physical form. Tom helped me evolve and understand this. The soul and essence of our being continues after death. It was difficult to believe that he loved me because I did not feel worthy of this angel filled with love and light. Somehow I realized that I felt he was better than I was. Never before had I received such deep love from anyone, and I couldn't understand how anyone could love me like that.

Cameron helped me believe that I was deserving and that Tom was assisting me to love myself and realize I was very loved. In truth, I didn't totally love and accept myself and couldn't fully open up to others. Tom loved me unconditionally, for just exactly who I was. Amazing. He said it was important to him that I believe him and that he didn't want to ascend until I did. He continued to express his deep feelings for me and pour out his love.

How could this be happening? When I stopped questioning and began simply to believe, I felt enormously blessed and felt the presence of Jesus. This experience was a gift from God for my healing. This helped me move closer to oneness with God. All of us can experience this level of love, but we must believe it is possible and heal from our wounds before we are able to open ourselves to receive it. I began to change. No longer could I question, deny, or mistrust this loving being. Doors opened wide inside me that had always been locked.

Tom's radiant love and light filled every corner of my being. The earthly term would be the radiance of love. That does not even begin to explain what I felt. There was an emergence of aspects of me I never knew existed that came from deep in my soul. This was unknown to me and seemed to be an awakening and transcendence to a different level of feeling and spirituality. The depth of our love was staggering; we became one.

His capacity for love and giving to me left me in awe. I began to know and deeply love this being who had inspired so many on earth. As I learned to receive and accept his love, I glowed and realized that his gift to me was to open me up to fuller dimensions of loving. I began to feel a change in Tom also. The more we shared our love, the more he opened to me. A heaviness lifted from him and was replaced by a serene peacefulness. He was no longer in a cage and his radiance seemed to intensify. He said that God had intended this for his deepening and healing. He said he felt whole and complete. After my life's journey, I could also say the same. Tom's loving energy continued to fill my life. My soul began dancing with joy for this beautiful being in my life who helped me to love and believe in myself.

Carole

All my life I have thought the male was the stronger one, not only in his body but in his mind. I always felt I could rely on the male in my life to take care of me. This was especially true with my father. Now that I think back, this must have been very scary for him. In the early years our whole family relied on him for support and many answers. I see very clearly now with his passing that he was weak and scared.

No wonder he became my betrayer. I pretended to be weak because that, I thought, was the thing to do being born female. He, in turn, took the power I gave him to fill the shoes I assigned for him. It's almost like he had to take control of me to exhibit his "fake" strength and not let me down. How very SAD. We both lost out instead of me keeping my own power.

I wonder how many times during my childhood I heard at home and in church, "Honor your father; honor your mother." Because I was so obedient, I did what I thought I should and gave much of my power away.

JOURNEY TO YOUR SOUL

Through most of my adult years, I gravitated to people who seemed to be stronger than me. Life seemed simpler that way. I let others make all the decisions; it seemed familiar and more comfortable. Long ago I learned that my opinions held no credence, so I adopted the policy of not caring much about anything. The truth is, I really did.

During therapy I realized that I did have a right to an opinion, just as much right as anyone else. But, I was still afraid of confrontations and hurting someone's feelings if I were to disagree with them. It was a slow process for me to make a shift and take these risks with another person. I've come to the conclusion now that a sharing of different opinions between people causes a deep respect for both parties, just the opposite of what I feared. As I have come to this knowing, I am taking more and more risks. If I feel good about the risk, my fan will be wide open in my heart-soul area. When I do this I always seem to come through the exchange empowered.

Channeling and writing this book is a huge risk. I understand there will be some naysayers, and that's understandable. I am gathering so much strength by doing this book, though, and it feels so right that I will continue on. When we started this project everything seemed just fine and exciting to me. Primarily loving words were emerging from Cameron. But by chapter three Father Tom Oddo was appearing through Nancy's hand. I was raised Catholic and felt the church doctrine would not accept channeling via Nancy's hand much less via my mouth. I became scared.

I really panicked when Father Oddo said he wished for a reform in his beloved Catholic Church. I was scared of the critics. I was afraid of any confrontation at all. As we got into more depth in the chapters, Cameron was also saying some profound things that could stir up some criticism. I wanted to go back to my old ways. I knew there I could be safe and far from controversy. I knew how to be weak and go into a cocoon. How could I possibly hold my own against people with much higher book learning and credentials? What could I back my inner knowing up with?

Somehow, somewhere I found the strength to finish this book without fear. All I know is it has given me such a wonderful expansion and such a feeling of wholeness that I can't stop. I feel I must be connecting with my male side that has been asleep until recently. I feel so secure.

It amazes me how I thought my strength came from others. Cameron told me when we started this book that my male-female energy would come into proper being. He even said that by doing this mission via the book, my male-female energy would move into alignment and serve me well. I didn't understand all that months ago. I now see that wholeness via male-female equality helps bring us all into our path of light.

TWELVE

Opposites Can Only Be the Same

Cameron

*H*ello again to our precious ones. My, we have a title that is confusing today, don't we? What does this title mean? Do you think this is some sort of a play on words here? Is that what you think? We could understand why. Today's lesson is very important! What we would like to say is for anything to be whole it has to have an opposite side to it. What could that possibly mean? How could that mean anything but non-sense? We will try to explain that today, to our precious and lovely students.

We would like to say what you are striving for in life is to have everything become whole. The only way for something to become whole is to have two sides, but they must be exact opposites of each other: hard to soft, hot to cold, angry to happy, fearful to calm. What does that all mean? How can that make sense? If you look in the dictionary, that isn't what it says. It certainly doesn't say these words mean the same thing. What does this mean?

We often see young children say something that seems clear, but they really mean the exact opposite of what they say. Have you ever noticed that? They will say, "I'm tired, I want to go home." When you take them home, they run like crazy all over the place. They weren't really tired. What was it they were trying to tell you? What does it mean when someone tells you something that really means something else? What are we trying to get at? We know that everything has to have two meanings, two sides, two opposites to become a whole. Of course, that is true of the male-female as we told you in the last chapter. But now we're talking about everything. Everything that you can think of in your entire world must have two sides to it.

As an example, for a beautiful flower to grow, let's say an elegant rose, in order to become whole, it has to open up, become a rose, wither down, and die. So what does that mean? It can be a beautiful rose, it can also be shriveled up and not pretty and it can also be ready to be clipped off and thrown away. What does that mean? To live is to die? Do you understand that? You are not whole until you are born and then you die. You cannot be whole until you die and go on. At this point we would like to go off the track and say that when you die in this world it is not really death. You never die. You are reborn, and reborn and reborn forever, for eternity. There is no death. We did want to point that out, and we will go into that in a later chapter. But our point today is that everything has to have an opposite side to it to make it a whole.

Shall we go to fabric? It has to start out hard to make it soft, or soft to make it hard. Let's go to the animal kingdom, and see what happens there. Let's say a puppy is born, a cute tiny puppy. They can be so cute and so lively. What happens to that puppy, how does it transform? It is sweet and cuddly perhaps, that puppy grows up to be an adult and because of circumstances and consequences it becomes a very angry dog and starts biting. It's not happy. It shows a fierce side, but it cannot be whole unless it has both sides, the sweet puppy side or the angry dog side. It would not be whole unless it had experienced, in some way, all of those different elements.

It is the same with humans, you know. You have to experience all the differences to make you whole. What would it be like if you went through life just smiling all the time, never a frown, never a conflict, just smiling. What would you learn out of life, very little indeed, I'm sure. What if you went through life and said, "I don't care. I don't have an opinion about anything." What would happen? What part of you would miss out that way? So you would have to experience having an opinion and having no opinion to become whole. Throughout life there has to be a flip side. We will even go to the material world, possessions. How would you know that you even have a possession if you've never had something? How would you know when you are rich unless you first didn't have any money? Do you see? You started out with no money, then you got lots of money, two sides again. You would not know you were poor unless you started to have money. It goes back and forth, back and forth. You have to experience one to have the other, to become whole.

We're not saying that you have to be poor and then win the lottery and then people will call you rich. That does not mean that money now makes you complete at all, that is not what we're saying. But how can you appreciate something unless you've had the opposite side of it? Without having the opposite experience, how can you ever appreciate anything? You need to always have an opposite to get a proper perspective, otherwise you only have one perspective on things. If you've never been ill, how would you know what it feels like to be well? You must know and understand both sides to become complete, to be a whole being. We are not saying you have to become ill to be whole. But what we're saying is you have to have at least a knowledge of the experience from your present or past life to know what people are talking about. That goes for anything, not just illness.

In school let's look at a small thing, perhaps grades. How would you balance that out? Let's say you get a proper high grade, an A, and you're feeling very good and elated. Then something happens next time, and you don't get an A, you get the opposite of an A, a failing grade. We don't like that word failing, but we want to have you experience the meanings. If you're an A, you're good; if you're an F, you're bad, is that what that means? That makes us so sad because nothing ever is a failure to us. To become whole you MUST experience or have an understanding that everything must have two opposite sides to become one. You see everything has a different side, everything has an opposite. When a candle is lit, it emanates an almost mesmerizing essence of beauty. When a candle is unlit, it speaks nothing, it just is. It's the same thing though, do you see?

We wish today to have you lovely ones understand that even though this might seem very confusing and not really necessary, we need to teach this most important concept of wholeness.

The biggest lesson we want to say is that you cannot be whole unless you come to earth and then come back to our side. You are whole in both places. We would like all of you to live to your fullest on earth, that is proper, that is good. But to be whole, you must then pass over and be on our side. It's almost like a revolving door. You go back and forth, back and forth, and you get so many experiences this way. Often, we see ones on earth thinking, well, on earth you are whole, you die, then you're gone. The opposite is really true, you know. Again you must have both sides. You must die to be reborn, reborn to die. That is the way it goes. Everything must be whole and complete.

Perhaps the next time you look at a butterfly, think of how much it goes through. But going through so much can only make it whole. It must get into a cocoon, you see, and when that cocoon opens, it is a butterfly. When it's time for the butterfly to leave, it's time will be up, and it will be gone. But without it being gone, it never really was, do you see? It has to be a complete circle to be a whole. This is the only way it is.

You may see someone on the street who is angry and in a situation that might make you a little tense. You could say to yourself, "That person is someone I do not want to be around because they are an angry type. I will not associate with such a person. I might stare at them though. They might even ruin part of my day and get me upset when I think about their anger." We want you to know that the person you saw was showing only one side of themselves. Their other side, the one that you did not see was soft. People cannot be whole unless they find their soft side too, their "unangry" side. Without anger and soft sides they would not be whole. That is part of what our mission is today, to try to get everything in BALANCE.

A good example of this is when you see a tree in the forest, think of that tree planted as a tiny seed and how it will grow up into a beautiful tree. But for that tree to be whole, it has to live its whole life, either by being cut down for lumber or maybe it's time for it to leave, die and go away. But without dying and going away or being chopped down for lumber, it has not served its whole tree purpose.

We hope this can bring some compassion when you see things happening around you. We hope you will not judge people or things so easily. Hopefully, you will know that at some point you are seeing them in a part of their cycle. Everyone you see on earth will at one time come to their full wholeness, whether it be this life or another life. So don't

127

judge how they are when you see them. Don't even judge so much as to say, "Well, that is an ugly flower." Please don't do that. What part of their cycle are they in? It is very important to get this concept. We wish for it to make sense to you that EVERYTHING IS IN A CYCLE WHEN YOU SEE IT, do you see? We often hear people on earth say, "Well, that person is very old, they would be of no use to me." Someone in a home for the aged doesn't get much credence. People sometimes think, well, their usefulness is gone. They have no use for me and I have no use for them. The opposite is true. You are just seeing them in a certain cycle in their life. We would love it if compassion could come through this chapter.

So when you see someone showing you one of their sides that may not be desirable to you, just know that they also have the opposite side in them. They can achieve that side by going on their path and finding their soul. You're always going to see an opposite to something, but just be aware that the cycle you see them in is EVER CHANGING, always different. They may be different just within a few minutes, you wait and see. Try to observe. It would be such a kindness not to judge others, not even to judge animals. Even little tiny flies that bother you, who might want to get into your food. You say, "Oh, those flies!" and you swat at them. But they have a time where they would not be a pest to you.

For everything living, we wish you to understand that their cycle is at a certain point in its path toward wholeness, and it IS SERVING A PURPOSE. If you come upon someone who you think is not doing proper things in your mind or doing a service to you, and you wish not to be around them, please think again. Let it be known that they are in a cycle just as you are in a cycle. Bless them for where they are. Bless them for their anger. Bless them for their yelling. Perhaps you see a larger yelling at a younger child, that is disconcerting, we understand that. That is a problem too that needs to be solved. But we just want to say, know that inside that person is NOT all anger. They can have compassion, they can be loving. Realize that the child has asked for that situation at that time.

Now that seems strange, doesn't it? More about that will come in a later chapter. But just know if you see a situation where you think someone seems out of control with another person, bless the situation. We are aware of it. This does not mean that if you see someone who is being harmed to the point of possibly a life being lost or a child who is being severely ridiculed that you shouldn't intervene. We're NOT saying not to intervene when someone is in danger. We are not saying that at all. What we are saying is, when you see BIG anger, observe before you judge. Observe and assess the situation. If you need to step in, that is proper and good, but some things take care of themselves, do you see? We thought we would just like to point that out if you don't mind.

We shall leave you with one point and that is we ARE aware, in the presence of our lovely God, of happenings that go on all the time on earth. What you see as harshness is being monitored by their angels. So you do not need to take this on as your duty and perform a conclusion unless someone is in danger, and then you will FEEL it. You will know if it is time to step in and then it will be proper, and you will be blessed at that time for that. But just know, we are watching all of our special ones. We will leave now.

Carole

As I walked out of Nancy's house after channeling this chapter and listening to the tape, my head was spinning. I could make very little sense out of the title, "Opposites Can Only Be the Same." I was sure Cameron had lost me with these words. As I looked down to step into my car, I noticed I was standing on barkdust; then I noticed the tree next to the curb. That was it, I felt it! The tree and barkdust are in different **forms.**

My awareness opened and as I drove home, everything I saw became a valuable lesson for me. I had fun seeing which cycle something was in. I really enjoyed figuring out how all these things started and in what form they were. Everything's purpose seemed more magnified to me.

When I started applying this theory to people, I felt such compassion. As I continued on in the week, I would see people in their angry mode and just know that inside of them was a softness. I found no need to stare or get upset at their wavering state; I just knew they were being monitored from above.

My deep healing, though, came with my father. I believe it would be quite a surprise to people who knew him that he had a side to him other than what his public face was. It's sad to note that his loving, calm side had such an unsettled flip side to it, shown to me so many times. Now I see he was trying so hard to find his wholeness. I have great comfort in knowing he will be able to come back here at some time. His spirit side did, in fact, tell me that he would be back on our side to complete some unfinished work for his soul. Hopefully, he will find his path of light n his next earth life so he can feel the wholeness, know the light and be of the light.

Nancy

If I hadn't experienced the full circle of opposites in my life I would not feel at peace as I now do. This has included cruelty and kindness, indifference and love, sadness and joy. For most of my life, I was numb and did not remember my early life experiences. My soul wanted me to remember now so that I would become real, find my soul, and become whole. I had to trust that I would be okay if I revealed myself to other people. I had to be brave enough, and I was.

It was necessary for my spiritual growth to feel a wide range of feelings as I experienced life's opposites. When we are hurt in life, we tend to shelve it to avoid feeling the pain. We think it would hurt too much. However, that very pain is the teacher that leads us to the deepest parts of ourselves. My pattern was to be happy all of the time so I could avoid facing myself. The truth is, I wasn't happy, wasn't at peace, and didn't have deep love in my life. Only when I allowed myself to feel the opposite feelings within me did I heal, deepen, begin to grow, and then experience deep love. The journey has been to the depths of despair where I did not want to continue. I had to visit that dark place and then slowly climb out and journey toward the light. It was hard. There was help all along the way if I was willing to ask for it. Never would I be able to feel the depth of the love and ecstacy I am now experiencing had I not allowed these opposites to emerge in me.

We are like a pendulum. In order for us to swing way out into love and light, we must have gathered enough momentum from being on the other side in despair and sadness. The deeper we are one way, the deeper we can go the other way. The pendulum can be in balance, but only if we work hard to get help when we are in despair. Some people's pendulums get stuck on the despair side and it never swings back. Do we have to experience sadness before we feel joy? Do we have to experience despair before we can appreciate ecstacy? Yes.

The wonderful thing I've found is that the more work I'm willing to do and the more I open myself to God, angels and people helping, the less my pendulum swings. It seems to be stopped now on the side of joy, love, and ecstasy instead of despair and sadness. I find it all gloriously amazing. Where is your pendulum? Allow it to swing and eventually yours will also stop on the side of love, joy, and peace.

Tom

I spent many years on earth observing people who were in love. There were endless hours in confession with people whose lives were torn apart because of their love for another person. Sometimes it was love for the person they were living with but unable to reach. They desired closeness and intimacy. Sometimes it was for someone they could not have. As a priest, I was a safe person they could express their turmoil to and ask for God's forgiveness for their weaknesses.

Why do we do that? Whoever said it is wrong to love someone and desire love back? We do not need to ask for God's forgiveness for this. Love is His gift to us, enabling us to feel deeply and experience all parts of ourselves. We should rejoice and thank Him for allowing us to awaken and become whole. Love can cause us pain, but there is growth through it as we become whole. It is an expanding experience to feel love, it reminds us of how empty and barren we were without it. Love is one of the most dramatic examples of opposites in our cycles that I know.

Most of us have experienced life without love. Then we fall in love and discover other parts of ourselves. In this experience there is a deep joy and deep sadness. We are always changed because of it. For some of us, love comes early in our cycle on earth, or in the middle, later in life or not at all. Can you imagine living an entire life and never even feeling love? This is the case for some. The truth is, all of us have opportunities on earth to experience love.

Some of us surround ourselves with armor and refuse to feel. We do not want to let anyone in. We're afraid we will be hurt or judged. I ask that you not operate on earth as a robot. That does not allow your natural cycle to run its course or for you to experience God's plan for you. We also tend to judge other people if they *do* follow their hearts. Our judgement is especially keen if they go against or flaunt societies rules. Perhaps it is loving a person of the same sex, perhaps it is loving a person who is married to another. You may not act on your feelings, depending on how willing you are to carry guilt for it, but please allow yourself to feel those feelings. Don't run away from it because you are afraid. You will discover beautiful parts in yourself.

Even opening and allowing ourselves to love our children deepens us. Why are we so afraid to express our feelings to our children? It is because we believe they will think we are weak. In reality, they respect us more when we are open and not afraid to express ourselves. Sometimes God brings us people to simply open us in preparation for someone else. The relationship could be a short one. If we do not allow these relationships for our learning, we must wait longer for our life partners. However, we should also understand that sometimes our cycle on earth is best fulfilled without a life partner.

Judging anyone and where they are in their cycle is not what God wants us to do. Who are we to impose our values and say another person is wrong for loving someone? Do we know what God's plan is for that person? Perhaps someone had an affair and we judged them for that. Please don't. They are in a certain cycle in their journey and they are deepening and growing. I promise you they judge themselves far more than you ever could. Individuals always change after that experience. They learn how to love on a deeper level and perhaps are able to bring this new self back into the original relationship and benefit that relationship. Perhaps they have grown and must move on. They all found, as I heard so many times, a difference in their ability to feel. Therein lies the opposite. They wouldn't be filled with such joy, in spite of their pain around it, had they not felt such absence of love in their lives prior to this new experience.

I saw death and birth, hate and love. I was a good and compassionate priest but never as fully until I experienced my love for Nancy. Finally, I understood how tormented one can be without the opportunity to give and express to the person we love. All of my senses intesified. What was happening to me? I didn't feel I had control over my life. My feelings for Nancy seemed to be taking over. That was very frightening for me. I was afraid of being judged. Of course, I would have been.

Do you know that I finally had decided, after over three years of feeling this way, that I needed to be whole and follow my soul to be complete? I was ready to give everything up and reveal my love to her. Nothing else seemed to matter. And yet, how could I leave my beloved church? I searched for an answer that would end my conflict. God allowed me to give up everything and be with Nancy, just not exactly as I thought. He wanted me to love her and heal from here and then to write to you in this book. It should not be necessary for priests to die in order to continue their cycles and grow.

God took me because of my mission now and because of the pain and shame it would have caused my church, the university, and my beloved friends and family. That would have been something I would never have wanted to do. How beautiful His plan was! How important my message is for my church leaders! How wonderful to be able to be with Nancy! No one in my life has taught me more, helped me believe in myself, nor loved me more than she does now.

I am ready for a shift in my cycle and sense it is coming very soon. Nancy has helped me heal from the shame I felt on earth for feeling as I did, and has helped me achieve a new depth in my feelings. Now I am ready for another opportunity to deepen. This will not be on earth; it will be in another dimension. I pray that you will be able to feel my love radiating to all of you through this book. I also ask God to love you and help you open your hearts and souls to all of the insights in this book. My request is that you do this so that you may also continue along your cycle.

THIRTEEN

Do We Die To Come Back?

Cameron

*H*ello today to our dear ones. We are in such delight because we believe that this book is going as it is intended, to the mission we have made for ourselves. Today we are going to introduce a concept that might be a little different to some of you. It has been slightly mentioned in previous chapters, but today we wish to expand on it a little bit. Do you think, and it is proper for many to think this way, when you die, when you come to our side, it is all over? Are you in a black hole? Are you in, perhaps, what you call hell if you think you are bad? Are you in heaven if you think you are good? We have a priest here who says there is something called "purgatory " to many he knew on earth. We don't know of purgatory. But he tells us it is a state of being in limbo when you are deciding how bad or how good you are. So you just have to THINK about where you will be. Will you be in heaven? Will you be in hell? That, he says, is a very simple term of what purgatory would stand for in words.

Today we would like to speak the total truth of what heaven, hell, and purgatory really are. We would like to speak of that if you would allow it. It might be necessary to have some really OPEN minds for this because some people may want to be in conflict with our ideas. We can only speak the truth from here. We don't even know how to speak an untruth. These pages are filled ONLY with truth, only truth from the soul.

We would like first of all to start out with the word "hell." What is that? Where did that name come from? We do believe it came from being misinterpreted from the Bible, from so long ago. We DO NOT believe there is a hell. When you think of the word, does that bring fire to your mind? Does that bring hotness? What does that bring to your mind? What has your religion taught about hell? We would like to tell you today that hell is only a state of mind that you have when you come to our side.

The word "hell"can be in your mind when you have the opportunity to review your life with your Creator. At that time, if you do not think you did the proper service that you set out to do on earth, you will then put your mind in a state, almost a dark state of not wanting to advance to the wholeness of the light. That light always has a draw to us here. You may have decided in your mind that you will be in a certain state. Possibly when you are in this state you will draw the conclusion that you will come to earth again to try to fulfill the advancement of your soul. If there was anything like hell here, that would be it. We will tell you that. There is no devil, there is no fire, there is nothing like that. That is an illusion.

We have a dear priest here who has spoken of purgatory. He says that is a state in which you decide whether you are

bad or good. There is no limbo purgatory state here. There
IS something we call the lullaby state. We think that would
be a better word. And that is when you are making a decision of whether to come to earth again or to ascend into the
light. We would like to call that the lullaby time. That state
has nothing to do with whether you've been bad or good,
nothing to do with that at all. It is a decision between you
and your Creator about where you would like to be.

   What people call "heaven" is a state in your mind when
you get over here that you have the right, almost the duty to
your soul, to ascend into the light that is pulling at you. If
you feel you have fulfilled the duties on earth that you have
proclaimed you have set out to do, you will then ascend
deeper into the light. There are many levels here. When we
say the word "level," we do not want your mind to go up or
down, that is not what it means, not less, not more, not at all.
People who are in a state of deciding if they should go to
earth because they have not fulfilled something are NO LESS
at all in spirit than people that are ready to ascend. It does
not work that way here, let me tell you that. Everyone is of
the same beautiful soul. They just have to complete more
lessons, that is all, there is no difference. Just because you
have decided to ascend to the light does not mean that when
you get there you cannot then decide to come down to earth
again or go to many other places, we want to tell you that.
Decisions can be made all the time. Nothing is written in
stone here, that is for sure, nothing is. There are always opposites, always opposite sides of what you can do, always
ever changing.

   We believe today, if we could have you know in your heart
that when you die, when a loved one dies, no one is gone.
You do not fall in a black hole. You do not go to heaven only
if you are good, you do not go to hell if you are bad. You
don't do any of those things. We want to say to you that the
only thing available to you or anyone IS heaven. Whatever

heaven conjectures up in your mind, the most beautiful thing, that would be the ONLY door open to someone who did even the most devious act on earth. We see those who are harsher on themselves than the Creator would ever be. That's why it is a decision between the Creator and the person coming to our side, where they shall go, which position they shall take, what they shall do. We believe it would bring great comfort to those who have deceased loved ones to know that they just don't go away. They come back or they ascend, or they go to other places.

Just know that when your loved ones come to our side, when you come to our side, a big greeter group is ready for you, I want to tell you that. Many people here who have touched your life will be waiting for you. You are never alone. They rejoice in your coming home because on our side, you are home. You are on earth because it can teach you so much, and you have chosen to do that. We glorify when you come to our side. We respect you very much for going to earth. Earth is hard, you know. There is much to learn on earth. It's a different energy on earth. Things are not easy on earth, we do know that. Just know your loved ones are well taken care of when they come to our side, just know that.

We often see people come on our side to take care of their loved ones on earth because that's the best way they can do it. They don't feel they have the power or the strength to be of help on earth. So they come to our side. That is true of our wonderful priest here. He chose his work on our side. He said, "I could do no more; I was powerless, I thought." He did much to raise his name in the church, we do see that. There was a purpose for that. The purpose was for the be- lieving. He knows, in his heart, credence would not have been as great from others if he had an unknown name. It was very hard for him, we see, to become almost as if he was on a pedestal on earth to many. He didn't like that. His soul be- gan to pull away and bind very tightly. He had a love, we see, that he needed to fulfill for wholeness. You see he is doing great work from this side in this book. We are blessed to have him. Just know when you come here, you will not be alone. We take care of you very well, and you take care of us. It is an exchange. We take care of your loved ones, as they take care of us. All is an exchange. But just know when you die, you do not go away, you are truly in the light and you are truly alive. We shall go for now. Bless you.

Carole

I am not positive how the Catholic religion views reincarnation. Although I was baptized Catholic as an infant and went to a parochial school for part of my primary grades, I still cannot tell you with much certainty what their teachings are on this. I do remember well the talk of heaven, hel,l and purgatory.

At the age of six or seven I tryed so hard to conjure up some sins that I had "done" so I could go to confession and my first communion. Confession, I learned, was the only key to communion. Communion was quite a highlight in our faith. The fancy, all-white dress and veil were a real draw for me as a little girl. I was nervous about confession. I remember I chose to make up sins so that I had SOMETHING to tell the priest.

Venial sins were not too bad, with mortal sins being the worst. I well remember something in me felt funny when I decided I had to lie and make up these sins to be able to go to first communion with my group. At six or seven, I really did not believe I was bad and had sinned, but it made me wonder. I remember being confused about lying to the priest about something I didn't really do. Somehow I passed that lying off as a venial sin, and hoped God would forgive me.

I do know this experience left many unsettled questions for me. The policy has hopefully changed in the forty plus years since my childhood. Today, I am not a practicing Catholic and so am not apprised of the current doctrine, but have heard there have been changes.

Even though I don't remember hearing the word "reincarnation" out loud, I do remember it was one of those hushed words that seemed curious, but never to be asked about. As I was growing up, I had some sort of inner knowing that made sense to me, and that was that you just don't drop into a big black hole when you die. I thought there must be something more. Hell and devils were something I never thought existed, purgatory, well, I was not so sure. And to get into heaven, my belief was that you must have to be especially good.

My awakening started with a most beautiful soul. Her name is Brooke. She is the daughter of a long-time friend. This friend blessed us by typing our manuscript. Brooke became ill at a very untimely young age. She passed over to the spirit side in her early twenties. She said her mission is to help us from that side. We have learned so much from her. As Brooke lay in her hospital bed in preparation for the ascent to the spirit side, I had the profound honor of sitting with her many times.

Her words confirmed that there was, in fact, an extraordinary side filled with so much light waiting for all of us when it is our time to pass over. When we spoke she seemed to be touching both spirit and earth sides at will. She came to "visit" me a few times after her passing. She allowed me to see her beautiful golden, long bouncy curls, her lovely face, and the silhouette of her body. She even wore "wings" to let me know for my own belief that she truly was an angel now. But it was her eyes, those magnificent eyes! She showed me that they had an unbelievable depth to them, a radiance that was far beyond anything I've ever seen on earth. The complete peace, contentment, and knowing that she showed were all I needed to confirm, without a doubt, that she was truly home now, very alive, and at total peace. Bless Brooke for her guidance and gifts. She is giving to so many of us who had the honor of knowing her on earth.

Tom

I grew up to believe that people who were sinful were destined to go to purgatory after they died. They were not loving on earth, so therefore they did not deserve God's loving radiance in heaven after death. This whole concept had guilt as its foundation. Guilt was supposed to keep people from sinning. Of course, we had already defined what sinning was, and I helped to explain that we all are sinners and that we must work very hard in life to be in God's good graces. As a child I knew that I should always serve God and try for perfection, but I accepted that I was sinful. This was so because I was told that all people are sinful.

Now I realize that no one is sinful really. God does not see this as we do on earth. He wants us to love ourselves and love each other. Those times are deep growing times for us. When we die, we judge ourselves for those acts, God does not.

When I reviewed my life after my death, I was shown my unloving acts through their feelings. I was shown how they felt when I was unkind to them. For some who have been cruel to others on earth, this is very difficult to experience. They truly understand how what they did affected others. For some, this is too much for them to bear, too much shame and guilt. They ask God to allow them to not come back to earth or ascend. They want to just be for awhile. They are ashamed.

This being state is what Cameron calls the lullaby state. It is a time when we have to come to terms with who we are and look at what we have done to other people and to ourselves. It gives us space to come to this awareness and then to be strong enough to want to change. Some then choose to come back to earth to serve others and try to pay back. Some are so filled with guilt that they ask to come back and experience pain and suffering to understand what it is like to be hurt by someone else, then realize and decide never to do that again.

My Lord has taught me that basing life on guilt is actually basing life on fear. We fear we will be punished or judged. This fear totally blocks the love that is available to us from God, Jesus, or any of our beautiful spiritual leaders who are our guides. Love cannot get in if fear resides within.

Does guilt really prevent people from sinning? Some, yes; most, no. God is asking us to operate on earth differently than we do. Instead of asking for forgiveness, He wants us to ask Him to be aligned with love and aligned with Him.

If we are angry, if we act unkindly to others, He asks that we pray for love in our hearts and for alignment with love. The focus on earth needs to move away from constantly asking for forgiveness. We already have it. To continually ask means we are fearful of being sinful and that we must try to obtain God's forgiveness. This fearful state prevents God's love from entering our souls.

Instead we must encourage each other to heal from our childhood wounds and to love ourselves. Many on earth did not receive adequate nurturing as children. This causes anger, lack of self-esteem, controlling issues, or total indifference to others as adults. Love and peace cannot get into these people. They act out to others because of the hurt inside of themselves. Or perhaps they cannot open up totally to others because they are afraid of being hurt. Their armor prevents love from getting in or from their love getting out. There are churches on earth who are teaching love with profound results in people's lives. They are helping people to heal and to realize we are all loved beyond comprehension. We hurt each other because we lack love of ourselves.

The purpose of our entire cycle is to learn to completely love ourselves and others unconditionally. For some of us, it takes a very long time and many lives to get to that point. When all the people on earth have a shift to loving, then existence will be based on giving and loving each other versus taking from and hurting each other.

Death is an opportunity for rebirth. It's a way station to help us determine where we've been, where we're going and how much love we have in our hearts. Love cannot reside where fear resides. When I died, I did separate from my body. Of course I have always believed in my soul as something separate from my physical body. What I wasn't prepared for was the profound love I experienced almost immediately from loving entities and my Lord on this side. Nothing on earth compares to this. Everyone who dies experiences this profound love.

I understood my mission and have acted as a guardian angel to Nancy on earth. I have been guiding and loving Nancy to help her to heal and awaken and find her soul. It was a glorious moment for me when she finally healed and evolved enough to connect with me. We communicate telepathically. All of you have loving angels guiding you. They speak to you constantly, but you can't hear. These are beings who have chosen to provide love and help to people on earth. For the last six years I have chosen to do that also. I felt I could help the best from here. I was the one guiding Nancy through her therapy and healing. She was smart enough to follow her instincts to get help. She listened and it worked. I was helping her find her soul. Her soul now guides her.

Soon I will be ascending; this simply means I will be experiencing more love. I will be filled with more light and love. The process leads us to oneness with God. God is filled with such profound love and light that it takes many steps before we are able to be one with Him. We have to learn to accept and believe this love.

I had no idea so much love was available to us. I felt Jesus's love for me on earth, but this is unbelievable. However, we must learn our lessons on earth or we aren't able to experience such a deep level where I am. We can't "skip" the earth steps. If we are on earth, that means our souls have chosen to be there to learn to feel and to give love. What surprised me also is that I feel here. I am able to feel and to grow. I didn't realize that the essence of who I am continues on.

I had to experience my love with Nancy so I would learn to feel at a deeper level. This allows me to ascend and feel the profound love that will be available to me. Feeling is the direct pathway to God. God is pure love. If we haven't learned how to feel, how is it possible to feel God's love on earth or here?

What awaits you here is magnificent. It's especially magnificent if you've learned how to give and receive love. Allow yourself those opportunities to open yourself up to those around you, you will feel more. Please don't be afraid. God will help you if you ask Him. If you believe He can help you, He will. Your rewards are beyond your wildest imagination. Love and joy to all of you.

Nancy

Never have I really believed in God, not as I do now with every portion of my soul. I've always believed in the concept of God and Jesus, but I viewed it all as an outsider. My angels guided me through my spiritual awakening, led me to the deep love that fills my life now, and helped me feel God, Jesus, and truth. I understand that I had to heal before I could feel any of this.

I had believed in the possibility of reincarnation, but I had never experienced anything that made me truly believe it. I had spent a good deal of time healing from my childhood, but I had no idea that I also had to heal from a past life. Now I see that this had been baggage that was getting in the way of my present life. With this realization I began to experience feelings from a past life. It was amazing!

At a workshop I met a man who shared similar spiritual beliefs. In the process of discussing our views within our small group, something literally clicked inside of me. This had never happened before. Joy overwhelmed me. I saw this person and instantly felt close. That evening I began to cry but had no idea why. It felt as if I had found a long-lost friend that I hadn't seen for eons. My only desire was to find out how he was.

Our paths crossed through work many times after that. Each time I felt an enormous bond to this person. I loved him dearly, and still had no idea why because I didn't even know him. Each time I was with him I simply wanted to go outside and run and play with him. "God, please tell me what this is!"

Several months after our first encounter, I was at a meeting with him again. As I left the meeting and was driving home, I got an image of a little girl about the age of ten. She had long brown braids and a pinafore dress (turn of the century type with the apron over the top). Never before had I been able to get images with my eyes open, only closed. This was very vivid; my eyes were open and it felt as if I was watching a movie while driving.

As I watched the little girl, I knew that her name was Molly. This Molly was the same man at the meeting. Beyond a doubt, I knew that it was the same energy and I could feel it. Molly was very, very dear to me, I could feel my love for her. As the images unfolded, I saw another little girl who looked just like Molly. Her name was Katie, and I sensed she was me; we were identical twins. We lived in a home with expansive lawns by a river. Molly and I played together constantly and were inseparable. Together we were one. The home had a wraparound white porch where we spent many hours playing. We had a fantasy world all to ourselves, even our talk was known only to us. We were filled with joy and love for each other twenty-four hours a day. I felt my love for Molly and the glorious feeling of being lost in our world together.

Then I saw Molly lying on a bed, she was very, very sick. I was afraid and could feel this fear now. Something was horribly wrong. Then she died. My mother pushed me aside and told me to go away. What did she mean, go away? This was my precious sister. My mom was so filled with grief that she couldn't deal with it. No one even talked about Molly's death and I wasn't allowed to go to the funeral. Everyone pretended it didn't happen.

I saw all of this now. My heart felt like it was being torn out of my chest. Molly, where are you? My images faded and I somehow made it home and began to cry. I cried for days. My feelings were of my life then, I felt myself as Katie. The joy and ecstasy of my life with Molly had been ripped instantly from me. I was devastated when Molly died, and I realized part of me also died. Deep grief and pain filled my soul as I began to realize that I never was allowed to grieve over my sweet sister, and had never gotten over the loss. In my past life I spent all my time looking for her and trying to fill the emptiness. Now I felt all of this. My love for her was so deep and, because she was my twin, I felt I had lost part of me. My life after her death was never filled with joy. I felt lost and alone. Now I simply allowed these feelings to come and released all of the tears that seemed to have been trapped in me forever.

As I began to heal I started to see things. In this life I saw that I have clung to people I loved too tightly. Now I understand that I was afraid they would die. When I lost Molly, I truly lost myself. I felt her sweetness all around me again now. She was the kinder, sweeter one, I thought. Slowly I began to realize that I really had Molly in my heart and soul, and I had never really lost her. Her kindness and sweetness were within me, I didn't need her to be present. What happened then was that I began to feel a part that had been empty before fill up. Rage spilled out at her for dying. How dare she leave me and our beautiful world together? I felt all of those feelings and was stunned. How could this be happening? Somehow I knew this was the absolute truth. Never could I have made this up as quickly as it unfolded before my eyes.

Time passed and slowly the hurt began to go away. This loss hurt me so deeply that I carried the pain into this life. My tears flow even now as I tell this story, I loved her so much. Now I do believe in past lives and reincarnation. One cannot experience these feelings and not believe. I had no idea that this pain was within me. A burden has been lifted from me. God presented this so that I could heal and move closer to being whole. I learned that I can be whole by myself and that no one else is needed to make me complete. It took two lifetimes to learn this lesson.

Thank you, God, for bringing this man to me as a vehicle to Molly and giving me strength to be able to release him and bless him on his path on earth. Thank you for awakening me to Molly, I will always carry her in my heart.

FOURTEEN

Do We Choose Our Own Path?

Cameron

*W*elcome again to our precious ones. Today we are going to talk about something that may in fact cause a little controversy as did the last chapter. We wish to say that people are in many different circumstances and experience many different consequences to things on earth. Oftentimes we see ones say, "Well, why me, why do I always have a problem? Why do I always get the short end of the stick? Why me, what is it that I've done?" Have you thought about that? Could we POSSIBLY suggest to you today that you might choose that path? You might have even chosen that path in a past life. Would that seem curious to you?

We wish to say that what we speak of is truth. You always have free will, that is for sure. You can always make a decision at the fork in the road. It's up to you which turn you choose to get there. You have come here to have a conclusion of your lessons in life and the conclusion will always be the same, no matter which road you choose to take. You have chosen circumstances, in agreeance with your soul, to learn these lessons well. Perhaps this was even chosen three or four lives ago, possibly something you needed to learn in this life that you chose not to learn in that life or in a previous life. Perhaps then you didn't have the strength. So this time you came here on earth to try again, to seek the challenge again. That seems strange, doesn't it?

How could we ever, ever ask for bad things to come our way? What is that all about anyway? Does it also seem curious to you when bad things happen to you that, in fact, they can end up being something good. When bad things happen to you, it really is a lesson of sorts that you've asked for yourself. You have asked for it to be drawn into your energy. We DO seek only goodness for ourselves, do you know that? But somehow to seek goodness you have to go through a path of darkness. In that way you have challenged yourself to learn more.

We do often wonder at young children when they seem to be on a path of near self destruction, self destruction by others, self destruction by themself. How can that be? How could a young child ask for that? Oftentimes we see the soul is seeking to learn something at a very young age. We see the Creator has given a definite way that young children can almost forget their younger years. That is a gift the Creator has given these young ones. Often we see people choose to have that challenge in their younger years because they know the Creator, in kindness, will let us forget and let us love as if nothing has happened. That is truly something the Creator has designed for young children. The Creator has blessed young children with this.

So when you see a young one in a situation that you feel is not desirable, think again before you step in and change that situation. Perhaps if you were to change it, what would happen is the young one would then again have to go through another learning process in another life to learn their desired lesson. This does not, of course, fall into this category if the child is in life threatening danger, that is not it at all. We're not talking about when you need to step in where an adult is doing physical harm. What we are talking about is a situation where a child is being berated for something, being punished for something that could be talked out in a calmer and better way. Just let it be known they've asked for this. They have asked for this fork in the road, maybe not in a conscious state of mind now on earth, but in the past it HAS been asked for.

We hope knowing this will lift a burden off of you. Sometimes when you see a situation that causes you dismay, just know that the angels again are watching. Your angels are always watching over you, and especially watching the little children. Their guardian angel is totally aware. We are aware of anything that is going on. We are aware when something is not in alignment. Just know if it becomes too bitter, too bad, the child will then be blessed by the Creator and will forget until the proper time of strength comes up for them to heal later. That is all we wish to say on that. But do know they are heavily blessed for any hard mission you see.

We want to touch again very briefly on the homeless. We have touched many times in this book on those ones. They have chosen this path, they wish for this path. They, perhaps, are filling a debt they think they needed to fulfill to add light to their soul. Please no need to feel sorry for them at all. Look deep into their eyes and just smile, that's all you need to do. If you wish to give a coin, that is proper for sure, but not necessary at all. They are not doing that to make you feel guilty, not at all. They are just fulfilling a mission. So do not feel bad for those you see in a circumstance of what you would call poor. We see many countries with many people in very deep poverty. No need to feel bad, that is their chosen path. They have asked for that. To you it would seem a hardship because you are not in that space. But you are in exactly what you have designed for yourself this life, nothing more, nothing less. So if that is truth, would it ever be proper to say, "Why me, why am I in this situation?" Just know your soul has asked for it but not your conscious mind. Your mind gets in it and mixes it all up and it makes no sense at all. Just know your heart has longed for that, your soul has longed for that, and you are playing it out. You are playing it out perfectly, you're always where you should be.

Shall we touch on illness? What is that all about? Why do we even have illness? We know this is something that is quite big on earth, as we've mentioned before. Illness gets a lot of duty on earth, we'll tell you that. People often bring illness into them for so many reasons. Sometimes they need to be cared for, they need to be loved. They will even bring an illness into them if they wish to leave earth. That is another vehicle to our side. Oftentimes that is the way it is done to get here. We look forward to the many, many, many, many years to come that illness will NOT be the vehicle to our side. Because that is not the way it needs to be, you know. Your Creator wishes for no suffering!

If you are aware of someone who is in a state of constant, constant illness, just know that the illness is serving a purpose for that one. You don't need to judge it. You don't need to do anything with it, it just IS. That is what these ones have asked for. So PLEASE, just be so patient with people and their ills and their ways. Be so patient. They have asked for that. They too are always in a constant state of learning. Their lessons would always be different than yours. It may become apparent to you that their path is very different than what you chose and that you might just need to even make a statement on it. That is NOT necessary, I will tell you that. Take that burden off of yourself. You're only responsible for your self, that is all. The best, best thing you can ever do for any-one who is in an ill state, a confined state, a poverty state, or anything that comes to your mind that would be different than you think should be, just bless them for their path. That's all you need to do. That is your only, only duty to them. Nothing more, nothing less.

I believe we shall go for now. I need to bless our lovely ones. Goodbye.

Carole

Long before Cameron channeled this book he said that the words in this book would be healing for Nancy, myself, and in turn, others. He gave us a choice whether we wanted to do this project or not. The choice was always ours. We de-cided to go ahead with the book. My feeling was, if it could in some way help only one person, the time would have been well spent. Cameron said we would also have a part in the book. Of course, neither one of us had ever written anything for publication. I couldn't imagine what I could write or how I could add to the book and even more, why would people want to read my words? What did I have to add to Cameron's words that would be of interest?

The only credentials for me to draw from are my heart and soul. And besides, I've done my therapy and deemed my-self healed, so why did I need it? But I continued on with our plans for the adventure. Well, I got quite a surprise as the book started to unfold. I may, in fact, write words that people do not feel so drawn to read, but I know for a fact that by doing my part in this book many areas were touched in my being that still needed to be addressed on a different level. By my revealing so much of myself on paper, getting it out, and really looking at an issue, the healing became in-tensely profound. I felt I was shedding layers as I wrote my part for each chapter.

My greatest comfort has come in this chapter, though. Sometimes I would wonder how different I would be if I would have had a loving, nurturing childhood. I would ponder so many ways it could have been better and happier for me. I'm now convinced I chose the path I traveled as a child. I feel blessed now that it turned out the way it did and that I was able to forget. God touched me in such a way that I had little memory until I was strong enough to face the issues and heal. I was able to go along even well into my forties and think all was well in those early years. I did wonder a lot about certain things, but I was able to change it to a happy thought without much trouble.

Because I chose to have my hard lessons very early, life now seems to be so easy, uncomplicated, and peaceful. My family and friends who now fill my life seem only to wish for harmony among themselves. We seem to draw strength from living a peaceful existence. What brings me the most joy now is to share feelings and thoughts. Hiding behind masks does not seem to be appropriate any more, ever. This is very different than my formative years.

I do believe this book has helped me come to nearly a full circle of healing. For me this can only come with total forgiveness of those who I think have done me harm in the past. I now understand they were only carrying out a mission of my wishes in a form that would teach me my asked lessons. They did this with their knowledge of the best way they knew how so I could continue on my journey to the light.

Nancy

Now I see how important my life experiences have been to my growth and deepening. My soul chose everything that has happened to me in order to find beauty and love in myself and in other people. I did not know my lessons while I was experiencing them, I had to learn and heal before I could see and understand.

When I finally began to like me and accept myself for who I am, that's when love came to me. Always I thought that I would have love when the right person came along. It's not that way. When we feel deep love within ourselves, by ourselves, that's when deep love comes into our lives. As we learn to love ourselves, we learn to forgive ourselves and others. When I experience life that involves pain, I know immediately that my soul is trying to get my attention to help me learn something and love myself more. Now I ask to be shown what the lesson is. It moves me very quickly through the pain or struggle.

Recently I had a lesson in accepting myself for who I am. Again I do not believe anything is by chance. My lesson came through a broken fingernail. I had decided to try artificial nails and much to my delight my hands looked beautiful. Continually I got compliments and I felt marvelously feminine. A great deal of energy was put into keeping them pretty. Then one day I accidentally ripped one of the artificial nails as well as my own nail partially off. I wouldn't be able to fix it for a month until it healed. Oh, now my beauty was gone. Only then did I began to realize how important it was to me to have beautiful, perfect nails and how important it was to me to try to be perfect in my appearance.

It seemed I always wanted a little more here and a little

less there in my figure, and more curl sometimes and less curl other times in my hair. It seems that this can become an obsession. I was rarely satisfied for very long periods. Slowly I began to see that I didn't need to be perfect. I began to love my body just as it was. My desire to change it began to go away. My false nails came off and I decided not to get a perm. I wondered if my love of weaving a little more blond into my hair would some day also not be as important to me. It was then that I felt more peaceful and accepting of myself.

Learning to find beauty and love in other people came through my career. I chose various jobs that enabled me to get to know a wide variety of people. Through work with homeless, low income, or disabled people, my eyes were opened to some beautiful souls. I didn't consciously know this when I chose these jobs. I see now, however, that I did choose this path. It provided me the opportunity to get to know the individuals and see beyond the physical form and find tolerance, compassion, and beauty.

My greatest gift was working with Special Olympians, individuals with mental disabilities. Some also have the double challenge of a physical disability. What I have found has stunned me: insights into human behavior, deep compassion, incredible wisdom in various areas, and love. I can remember a girl so deformed people were repelled by her. God has given me X-ray vision to see into the souls and beyond the outer appearance. I was drawn to her and saw a radiant soul. I took her face into my hands and told her she was beautiful. She was, she radiated love and I could feel it.

People with mental disabilities face unbelievable obstacles in learning to love themselves. Their minds and bodies don't do what they want and they get frustrated. Often people are cruel and judgemental of them. They are treated as if they are not human and do not have feelings. I spent endless hours listening to their joys and worries and treasured each moment. They were willing to be open with their emotions. I valued their honesty and lack of fear. The purity of their feelings was humbling and valuable. Their lack of inhibition was beautiful. These individuals are teachers for us and deserve to be honored for the difficultt burdens they've taken on.

When I judged other people, I believe it really was a signal that I was not happy with myself. I have chosen numerous experiences in my life to teach me this. The more I loved and understood myself, the more I loved and accepted other people. That's what unconditional love means.

The interesting thing I have found is that when I got to the point of feeling unconditional love for others, I was the ultimate winner, not them. At that point I was at peace, happy, and I loved myself. It was then that my life was filled with more love than I thought possible.

Tom

It is my belief that I chose exactly what my life on earth was to be. Now I see that from my pain as a child, I found God, and from my love of Nancy, I found myself. My love of her now is without pain or shame, it fills my soul. She has been a precious gift to me.

I suffered a great deal of pain on earth. What I would like to explore is whether or not pain is the only avenue to deep feeling and a deep relationship with God. I believe I have chosen everything that has happened to me on earth and now. The choice was mine with my Creator for my growth. I'm here now to suggest that it is not God's intention for us to suffer pain. It is not necessary to grow just that way. God would like us to grow through love instead.

Pain and suffering are a regular way of life for many on earth. For many, the pain creates anger and a closing down within us that often results in causing pain in others and prevents love from filling our souls. Pain has escalated on earth to the point of almost being out of control. Violence is a symptom of the pain on earth.

On earth I chose the experiences of my life to experience the pain. I also chose to experience love. I see it was my research for this book, in addition to my deepening. I've grown far more through my relationship with Nancy, free of constraints, than I did my entire life on earth in self-sacrifice and pain. When I refer to growth, I mean awakening feelings, finding my soul, and moving closer to God. I looked at the differences in me so that I could truly believe how profound love is for our growth.

It takes a conscious choice by each of us to choose love instead of pain. There are many souls now on earth who have come back as teachers to help the earth shift. The messages are bombarding earth through books, movies and workshops. For the shift to occur, however, each person must develop love in their soul instead of fear. Pain is really fear, you know. When you eliminate all fear from your life, then you eliminate all pain. The result is love all around you. You would not be reading this book unless there had been a shift in you already, however small or large. Your soul has chosen that in this life you will open up and begin to love more. That is infectious to all around you and spreads. When you choose love instead of fear and pain as a reaction to situations around you, then there will be peace on earth.

The purpose of this book is to help you find your soul and then to be guided by it. Your soul has already chosen this as your path, it is simply playing out. We have attempted to teach you that your journey is one of learning how to feel. Feeling leads us to feeling God within us and helps us progress in our cycle.

My soul chose to love on earth as a way to grow. However, I was in a situation where I felt I could not follow my soul and experience that love on earth. I didn't see a solution that would allow me to experience love and be free. My main mission through this book is to ask for priests to be free. Many desire freedom, you know. It is an unnatural state they are forced into. It is God's will that this change. Lessons through loving are more profound than those through pain and self-sacrifice. We have discussed the necessity of experiencing opposites in our cycles and the importance of the pendulum swinging back and forth. Most people on earth are stuck presently between pain and less pain or uncomfortable times and low levels of loving and sharing. I often heard on earth that life is about struggles and nothing is ever perfect. I'm here to tell you life doesn't need to be about struggles. However, you have to break free of the old way of thinking that you cannot have what you want from life. You can have everything from life and more.

The opposites between which you swing back and forth can be between loving and profound loving. That is truly a shift from the continuum that includes pain. Your ability to reach this new continuum of deeper loving is limited now because of the fear that is on earth. You are not reaching the higher levels of love that are available to you because you fear to truly open yourself to other people and express your feelings.

Do you know how to express your feelings? Do you have feelings that you can identify? Are you afraid to express your feelings to those around you? Do you have deep passion in your life with those you love? Passion comes with opening ourselves to others. Perhaps you're not getting love back in your relationships. It may be time to allow those who are not loving you to go on their own path, separate from yours. Love yourself enough to believe you deserve more love in your life. You can create and choose a life that is more loving.

If you do not have love in your life, perhaps you are afraid to draw people to you. Angels are all around you to help you. Ask God to open you to the love and guidance that is available to you. Please have the courage to take some risks. Tell people you love them. You can experience on earth the love I am experiencing here. It's about allowing the love to reach you once you've eliminated your fears. The choice is yours.

Love and peace to all of you.

FIFTEEN

For Now
We Say
Goodbye

Cameron

We are now at the conclusion of our book. We have certainly been on a journey, haven't we? You are all so precious and dear to us, it is sad to leave you. But it will not be for too long. We wish to have another book coming in the future. This will not be by me, nor in Tom's hand. This will be by another angel. She is of a higher degree in being able to teach. My job was really to set the pillars down, set the foundation. Our lovely priest wished for a reform in his church. He wished to put pillars down also, a foundation for change. We think he did that quite well indeed.

We wish at this time to thank these two ladies who have written this book. Did you know this was, in a sense, a fearful time for them? We know it's a big risk for them to put this book out on the shelves. But we feel that their souls are so expanded by this that they will do it.

It is our hope that an opening in many souls has come through this book and a seed has been planted. We wish to give thanks and bless people very highly who have read this book, who have attempted to open their souls. It has to start at the soul level, you know. The journey will be so wonderful, so beautiful, and so very powerful, beyond your imagination if you would go through life from now forward with your fan open, with your heart open, with your soul open.

We also wish to say to our most precious and lovely students that I shall be leaving soon. Our wonderful priest shall be leaving soon also. We need to go on to other missions. Our mission was in this book, that is for sure. But we leave with a heavy heart, for you have become our precious ones. Just know that we are always guiding you, always watching you from above. Our mission is only for your wholeness, that is all. And we hope we've been able to create an opening, create a little slit behind the eyes to open the soul. If we have done that, then we can proclaim we have helped.

Please all go in peace, for we love all of you. We especially love these two brave women who have brought this book forth. They are highly blessed for this. We shall go for now and peace be with you always.

Cameron and Guides

Carole

It is hard to believe we have come to the end of this book. After I was through channeling Cameron for the final chapter, Nancy and I just looked at each other and wondered what lies ahead.

This book has consumed a fair amount of our thoughts and time in the last several months. Nancy and I were always trying to arrange our schedules with our families in mind so we could have some time to ourselves to record another chapter. My portable cassette player traveled many places with us so we could grab an hour here or there. These chapters have been channeled many places, at the park, in our vans, while our boys practiced soccer, as well as before and after games, early mornings before Nancy goes to work, late evenings after work. Weekends seemed to work out best and became a favorite time for us.

Cameron has helped us so many times. He has answered our questions while we were talking on the phone. He sits with us at Nancy's picnic table under her huge fir trees, he also joins us outside on my deck while we're enjoying the sun. He travels with us on any outing we take together. He has become a constant companion for Nancy and myself for so long that I know a huge void will be felt by us when he leaves. I now feel so blessed that he left us with his wisdom expressed on these pages.

I did not have the privilege of knowing Father Oddo while he was on earth. Nor did I know that he was the beloved president of the University of Portland. Now however, I feel I know him well through his writings and am so very honored to have his loving and inspiring words in this book.

Channeling seemed a bit of a mystery to me. More than a few times I have gotten my head into this book and not let my heart guide me. When that happened, I became scared, so scared that I couldn't make any sense at all of how this could be happening. Only when I put my "head on the shelf" and let my heart-soul lead, could I continue on.

It astonishes me now how much faith, though, I have put into my heart and soul. I have reached the conclusion of this book with a deep trust in my own inner knowing. I feel now, without a doubt, that all these words are only pure truth. To have done this seems like quite a leap in spiritual faith for me. I have quit asking "Why me,?" and just accepted this as a mission I must have asked for on some level.

I now offer my love and supreme thanks to the most precious of angels, Cameron and Tom. I also wish to thank Brooke for opening the door to the other side six years ago, thus allowing me to consider and know for myself that angels DO in fact exist, and that they are there to help guide us if we just choose to listen.

The grand design for each of us seems to have a way of unfolding even when we're not looking. Last evening I received the news that my mother made a very peaceful transition to the other side. I am humbled she chose to pass over so quietly.

This book is now a short time away from print. My concern with the release of this book was that the words enclosed could add to the burden my mother already seemed to be carrying. That has now been erased. I am no longer fearful of this.

Mother is now free of her pain and suffering. Her bondage to earth has vanished. The play is done, the curtains are drawn. Every scene chosen by my parents to act out in this life are over. Many scenes were so difficult. They preformed their parts so well that I was able to become strong, seek my path, and, most importantly, be who I really am. Bless them for that! May their souls rejoice, for they are home.

Carole

Nancy

I decided to write my last chapter on my camping trip near beautiful Mt. Hood in Oregon. Awakening early, I saw dew on the tent and heard forest sounds stirring. I feel comfortable. Because this last chapter is difficult for me, I wanted to be somewhere where I felt nourished by beauty.

The end of this book signifies the end of the most fascinating journey that I have ever been on. The journey to find our soul culminates in more fulfillment than any journey on earth could possibly provide. I feel that I've been on a long quest, in search of the treasure of love and in the process, I conquered the childhood demons and dragons that prevented me from having this love.

It's not really the end but rather the beginning now that I've found this path. I'm excited to discover more about myself and the love within me and feel extremely lucky to have had these marvelous experiences. My love and gratitude to Cameron is beyond measurement. He has guided me to find my soul, trust myself, and trust God. With each chapter something would happen to me to deepen me or heal me, as if I was to live the lesson in order to share my experiences with you. That's exactly what happened and it all amazed me. Carole experienced similar lessons at the same time so that she could write about them too. We lived parallel lives as our angels prepared us for the book and helped us grow.

Cameron taught me how fear causes us to fuss and fret over things at work or home because we're worried things won't work out. Enormous amounts of energy go into this and cause great stress for all of us. Cameron taught me the concept of abundance. Believe and trust that things will work out, and they do. Ask God to help guide you to solutions, and God does. Believe that you will have abundance in your life, and you will. If you believe, fear won't be your partner and prevent the miracles.

As a single parent on a salary that doesn't meet my expenses each month, I've had to learn to trust that I would be okay. When I was desperate to pay a bill, Cameron said ask God to help you and then get quiet and listen for your guidance. ALWAYS I found a solution.

For people who are not believers in the powers of the universe, I understand a possible disbelief of my words. Now I know that when I stopped trying to figure everything out by myself and began to ask for help from God, the help came pouring my way. I've heard people say that it is weak to ask for help and not be able to do things by ourselves. I've learned differently.

Those who ask for help are the ones who are strong and courageous. It's about surrendering the struggle and trusting that someone or something has a better way of running our lives. It's about getting quiet to listen for our guidance. It's also about continuing to trust even if the abundance does not come when we think it should. It will come.

I can't explain for a minute what the power is that I've surrendered to, to guide my life. I call this power God. Whatever it is, since I've surrendered to that guidance (and I don't make any decision without first consulting my inner guidance), I've discovered abundance, deep love and peace. I've gained great power in my life. I thank Cameron for leading me to this beauty within me and helping me to trust and be guided by it.

The end of this book also means that Tom will be ascending and will not be as close to earth. Will I have enough strength to let him go? Many times my heart aches and my tears flow. The beauty, wisdom, and love in him is beyond description. I cherish him and cannot imagine my life without him or without the love we share. When I ask Jesus to help me with this, I feel Him lift my pain.

Tom has filled volumes of pages helping me to understand that people don't leave once they die. They are always within us. Once we have connected on a deep soul level, they are always within us.

Tom said he would come back to me someday, but that he is being guided to grow and gain more love. He says that I will grow as he grows because I will feel his deepening and deepen myself. We are one, he says, and deeply connected.

I understand that I wouldn't be experiencing this grief if I wasn't in transition and growing. We both are evolving and are helping each other with this transition. There always is uncertainty in change. We both are growing in our trust as we believe the next step will be filled with even deeper love. He says that he wants me to experience love with someone on earth. Loving from different dimensions is too difficult for both of us.

I feel loved and cherished for the first time in my entire life. Tom has taught me to love and believe in myself. He has awakened love within me and helped me heal. The more I am willing to share my feelings with him, the more love I feel.

I've pondered over the beautiful miracle of all of this. So often I have heard men on earth say that they do not understand what women want. Women and all people desire deep down to be loved and cherished. I do feel loved and cherished by Tom and I am fulfilled. It is interesting to me that he has done that without touching me, buying me a gift, or taking me anywhere. He has done this through his beautiful words. He expresses how he feels about me and tells me over and over again. It's what we say from the depths of our souls that creates deep love in our lives. It's the willingness to reveal who we are and how we feel.

Sometimes we look for the perfect gift for those we love. We already have that perfect gift. It costs nothing. That gift is ourselves. The expression of ourselves, our heart and soul, what we are feeling or are worried or joyful about is what kindles love in our relationships. The more we are willing to do this, the deeper our love goes.

What an incredible gift Tom has been to me. I am such a different person since he came to me. I struggle deeply within as I release him and deepen in my faith that this is a necessary part for the deepening of our relationship. Sometimes the best and most beautiful gift for a relationship is to let it go for now. My love continues for my beautiful angel, Tom.

Nancy

Tom

Goodbye for me is difficult. I will not be gone forever when I ascend, but nevertheless, I will not be hovering near earth as I have been for the past six years. I will be growing through immense love. Someday in the future I would like to come back to Nancy, connect again and speak to all of you about my new journey. All of us wonder what life is like after death. My continuing mission with Nancy throughout her life on earth is to share with you as I grow and learn. Death is not something to fear. It is a glorious opportunity to begin again and move to higher and higher levels of loving. The more I can share with you, the more I can help dispel fears on earth. I want to help bring about the shift on earth to more loving. This book, and similar ones, are providing the opening to a deeper spirituality on earth.

I am immensely grateful to my Lord for taking me when He did. I did not break my vows on earth. I never would have been free of guilt and shame with Nancy on earth. This way our love is pure. She is not married and I am free. This is such a beautiful lesson for me in trust. Throughout all of my pain on earth and desire to be with Nancy and be free, I always had faith in God's plan for me. Somehow my faith allowed me to endure. Never in my wildest imagination would I have envisioned writing a book with the woman I love and finally being able to express my love to her. And I am in a place filled with light and love and endless opportunities.

God and my soul wanted me to publicly express my feelings. This necessitated that I be very strong and believe in myself. I have had to grow a great deal to be able to express my feelings about my church and Nancy. For a priest this is courageous. I see the beauty of it all. I had to have courage and love of myself, even from here, to be able to override the feelings of shame and guilt. You see, when you come over to our side, you retain the basic feelings you feel about yourself. Many of your fears are washed away because of the overpowering love on this side, but you have to face you. The questions each time are how much do I love myself, how much do I love other people? You decide what the next lessons will be to allow you to become more loving. So the essence of me came here. My ability to understand everything is amplified. It's a knowing I receive.

When I died, I knew that someday I would connect with Nancy and be able to express my feelings. I guided her from afar and simply waited. It's been almost ten years of earth time that I've loved her. I am totally different than I was ten years ago. I feel whole and loved and cherished. I feel healed from my feelings of shame. My soul knew what would happen to me when Nancy finally awakened and could hear me. I would experience that wonderful opportunity in our cycle when we receive back what we give. Nancy has an enormous capacity for loving. I am extremely lucky to receive her deep affection and be able to connect with her joyful way of being. It fills me up where I was barren before. It has taken me this entire time, however, to be able to learn how to receive. As a priest I always denied my needs and felt I should be the one giving. I know many attempted to give love back to me on earth, but I felt uncomfortable and couldn't receive it. It's all about getting rid of the fears we have. Possibly we are afraid of our own feelings when we really do let people give to us. We feel at times that we might be overcome by emotion and not be in control anymore. This is a barrier to friendships and deep relationships.

This book has helped heal my fears. As I had the courage to reveal my feelings and fears to Nancy, I was able to accept her fears and feelings also. The intensity of her love for me was hard to accept. Receiving is often hard for men on earth. I saw that many times.

I am struggling the most with not wanting to leave her radiant love. I have only just found this beautiful being and now I must follow my Lord and move on. I have tried many times to write this chapter, but I could not. I was filled with grief. You see, I also have a broken heart, even here. I believe we were to experience each other for healing and development of our whole loving selves in preparation for another profound step in our cycles. I'm beginning to sense the next level and I am deeply humbled.

Change is difficult for all of us. I will be back. So many of you are shifting and loving more in your lives. I feel it and see it. It takes courage to walk a different walk and believe differently. It takes trust and faith. If you haven't found God and Jesus, try saying a prayer asking that they be revealed to you. Simply asking changes you. I ask that you stop the busyness of your daily lives and get quiet and talk to God. Our Creator is always listening, we are the ones who question because we can't hear.

Love is waiting for you on earth. Deeper love than you have now. Nancy has shown me a deeper way of loving. Please be open to the messengers of love that come to you, for they are your opportunity to deepen and move closer to finding who you really are, finding God and developing a peace that envelopes you.

Much love to all of you as you began your journey to your soul.

Tom

Journey To Your Soul
The Angels Guide To Love And Wholeness
is available from your local bookstore

Distributed by
Associated Publishers Group
Nashville, Tennesee
800-327-5113

Published by
White Phoenix Publishing
P.O. Box 2157
Lake Oswego, Oregon 97035
503-639-4549